Performance Conversations®

An Alternative to Appraisals

Performance Conversations®

An Alternative to Appraisals

Christopher D. Lee, PhD, SPHR

Published by Fenestra Books™
610 East Delano Street, Suite 104, Tucson, Arizona 85705 U.S.A.
www.fenestrabooks.com

ISBN: 1-58736-605-3
LCCN: 2006921666

TABLE OF CONTENTS

Fallacy A: performance appraisal is the only process organizations use to describe, measure, and evaluate individuals' contributions.

Fallacy B: The primary goal of performance appraisal is to measure and rate performance.

Fallacy C: A well-designed performance appraisal system will always work as planned.

Fallacy D: Performance appraisal and performance feedback are one and the same.

Fallacy E: Appropriately designed incentives will motivate employees to perform better.

Fallacy F: Rating (or grading) performance is sound management.

Fallacy G: Performance appraisals are a necessary evil.

Acknowledgements

For Don Harward, President Emeritus of Bates College, whose conceptualization of a quasi-performance management process called the "conversations document" provided me with the intellectual stimulation to prove what I already knew at my core—people want feedback, not appraisal.

Dozens of friends and colleagues were consulted in the development of the ideas that produced this text. Most notably, and in no particular order of importance or depth of contribution, I would like to recognize Robert Bremm, Shirley Govindasamy, Jaffus Hardrick, Brian Hill, Scott Keenan, Peter Martel, Sarah Potter, Greg Shropshire, Giles Strickland, Neil Strodel, Robert Tetreault, and my former colleagues in the Bates College Human Resources Department. Also, recognition goes to my students, who educate me more and more each semester: Roberta Sherwood, Jared Avery, and Jim Catevenis. And thanks to the world's best editor, Maureen Elgersman Lee, who worked tirelessly for meager wages—none—to make this the best book possible. Finally, recognition for the late Professor Philip Benham, a true scholar and gentlemen, whose review of an early draft exploded my view of my own work and encouraged the completion of the book. I hope that he would be proud of the result. Look, Mom, my second book!

How to Use This Book

Why You Should Buy This Book

IF YOU DREAD THE annual performance appraisal process, invest in this book. You will learn a revolutionary process to track, monitor, document, and improve your subordinates' performance.

Who Should Read This Book

Managers/Supervisors. The Performance Conversations® model will give you tools to coach your employees to peak performance while still meeting the administrative requirement of many organizations to produce annual performance appraisal documents.

Human Resources Professionals. Those who are responsible for performance management systems can use this book to audit and improve their current performance systems. Most importantly, after learning the benefits of the Performance Conversations® model, you will decide to replace your current system. Tools and techniques to better train supervisors to manage and document individual performance will also be provided.

Senior Leaders. Chief executives, vice presidents, general managers, and those responsible for large enterprises will benefit from advice on developing an organizational culture that drives individual performance.

What Is in This Book

This book contains three major components:

1. An introduction to the Performance Conversations® model of performance management.

2. A critique of traditional appraisals.

3. A guide to twenty-first-century supervision and management techniques.

The topic areas included are as follows:

- how to avoid the fifteen fallacies of performance appraisals.

- why feedback is superior to appraisals.

- why *conversations,* not *evaluations,* are the key to successfully coaching performance.

- how to integrate supervision and performance management tasks.

- managing behavior, conformance, and performance.

- why and how organizational culture drives individual performance.

- introduction of the angle theory of feedback.

- how to use the Performance Conversations® model.

- pay alternatives that support twenty-first-century approaches to management.

How to Read This Book

The best way to read this book is in the order that it was written! ☺ However, busy managers who are eager for the solution should read chapters 1–3, the quick reference points at the end of each chapter, and then skip to part III. Part III (chapters 8, 9, and 10) comprises the how-to portion of the book. Part II presents the full argument as to why you should *never, ever* use traditional appraisals to manage performance.

Website and Other Resources

The website at www.performanceconversations.com is an ever growing resource on the subject of, and solutions to, more effective performance management. It contains tools, sample forms, newsletters, articles, a bibliography, and other resources for managers and supervisors.

I would be very interested in your experience with the Performance Conversations® model. There is a feedback section on the website, so please take an opportunity to share your thoughts and experiences. You can also write to share any horror stories about your past experience with performance appraisals.

I wrote this book because I am passionate about human performance. It is my hope that you are inspired to make performance management changes in your organization.

Fallacies, Truths, and Solutions

Fallacy A: The performance appraisal is the only process organizations use to describe, measure, and evaluate individuals' contributions.

Truth: The performance appraisal process is only one part of a larger system that regulates performance.

Solution: Design, adjust, and manage the organization as an interdependent system that supports performance. Integrate HR systems to include performance management and align all performance management initiatives with the organizational culture and environment.

Fallacy B: The primary goal of the performance appraisal is to measure and rate performance.

Truth: The real goals are to sustain good performance, improve performance, or correct poor performance.

Solution: The performance management process should be future oriented and focused on information, feedback, and description rather than measurement, evaluation, and documentation.

Fallacy C: A well-designed performance appraisal system will always work as planned.

Truth: A process that is not used (or used improperly) by managers and employees is useless.

Solution: Hold supervisors accountable for their staff development, supervision, results, and participation in the performance management process (completed, on time, and accurate).

Fallacy D: Performance appraisal and performance feedback are one in the same.

Truth: Appraisal is judgment; feedback is useful information.

Solution: Formal, informal, ongoing, periodic, micro-level and macro-level feedback should all be used to manage performance.

Fallacy E: Appropriately designed incentives will motivate employees to perform better.

Truth: Motivation is intrinsic; extrinsic motivation has very limited effectiveness.

Solution: Providing challenging, meaningful work; creating a nurturing and supportive environment; and involving employees in decisions that affect their work—these imperatives encourage pride in workmanship and personal growth. This is the key to sustained motivation.

Fallacy F: Rating (or grading) performance is sound management.

Truth: Ratings reflect Theory X management.

Solution: Abandon the use of ratings, and emphasize description, diagnosis, and discussion instead.

Fallacy G: Performance appraisals are a necessary evil.

Truth: Many well-run organizations do not have a formal method of performance appraisal.

Solution: Do not use traditional performance appraisals.

Fallacy H: Appraisals are necessary for documentation and administrative decisions.

Truth: Appraisals and documentation *are not one in the same thing.*

Solution: Other management systems can be used to document performance and meet administrative requirements.

Fallacy I: Supervisors are omniscient, they see and know all.

Truth: Supervisors do not see everything, miss some things, and often take vacations.

Solution: Train supervisors very well in the science of supervision and require employees to be highly involved in performance management process.

Fallacy J: A well-trained supervisor can overcome rater bias.

Truth: Most of us are human.

Solution: Either hire androids, or abandon the use of rating systems and require employees to be involved in the tracking of their efforts.

Fallacy K: Supervisors and employees see value in performance appraisals.

Truth: Rarely are kind words spoken about the performance appraisal process.

Solution: Abandon the use of traditional performance appraisals.

Fallacy L: Appraisal instruments contain all the important dimensions of performance.

Truth: It is not possible to account for all performance dimensions for all positions and for all types of employees on any single appraisal instrument.

Solution: Performance management systems should consist of a *process* versus a form with a narrowly defined purpose—performance improvement.

Fallacy M: Appraising only performance factors is enough.

Truth: Bad behavior undermines good performance.

Solution P: Behavior, conformance, and performance should all be managed within the performance management process.

Fallacy N: Progressive discipline occurs inside of the performance appraisal process.

Truth: Discipline should not occur within the performance management process.

Solution: Progressive discipline and discipline without punishment should occur separately from the performance management process.

Fallacy O: Performance appraisal is a reliable basis for making administrative decisions.

Truth: There at least 15 flaws attributed to performance appraisals, any or all of them undermine the administrative decisions based upon their use.

Solution: Abandon the use of traditional performance appraisals.

PART I

The Argument

I hate performance appraisals. They work against the very thing we desire—improved performance. Peter Block, W. Edwards Deming, Phillip Crosby, and Steven Covey harangue against them, and if they can't change organizations' fascination with this annual bloodletting ritual, I don't imagine my words will help either. Nonetheless, I'll try.

—Rick Maurer

Introduction: According to the Experts

Performance appraisals seldom, if ever, work as advertised. Appraisals do not work because they are fundamentally flawed in their design, use, and intent. They work against human nature, contain false assumptions, and are founded upon outdated theories. In fact, embedded in almost every single book on the subject is a chapter, a few pages, a table, a paragraph, or a few sentences that are essentially disclaimers. These disclaimers describe the conditions, circumstances, or occasions when performance appraisals may not work. Taken as a whole, the problems of performance appraisals cannot be overcome.

There are hundreds of books about how to do appraisals, how to do them better, or how to do them differently. Organizations are always in the process of implementing new and better systems. The new systems replace old systems that did not work as expected. The average performance appraisal system lasts only three to five years, and then the virtually endless cycle of selecting, implementing, and replacing the system is repeated. The reality is that performance appraisals as practiced in the vast majority of organizations simply do not work.

Many organizations blindly use them in a misguided attempt to motivate employees to perform better. Yet, appraisals were never designed to improve performance, only to measure and rate it.

Managers and employees dislike appraisals and everyone knows that they are not good for morale. Appraisals are known for being inaccurate and for causing fear and anger. This certainly outweighs any good that they might create. Appraisals are a prehistoric method of managing and motivating employees.

Performance appraisals were built for an industrial world. Organizations would be wise to abandon the use of this outdated system that never actually worked. The Performance Conversations® approach is the right solution for the twenty-first century.

The inherent problems of performance
appraisals cannot be overcome

The Experts Agree, Don't They?

Here is a small collection of observations about the limited worth of appraisals by authors who are for and against their use (an amusing exercise would be to guess which is which):

> Some have argued that all performance appraisals systems are so flawed that they are manipulative, abusive, autocratic, and counterproductive.
> —Noe, *Human Resources Management*, p. 329

> Management by objectives and performance appraisal processes, as typically practiced, are inherently self-defeating over the long run because they are based on a reward-punishment psychology that serves to intensify the pressure on the individual while really offering a very limited choice of objectives.
> —Levinson, "Management by Whose Objectives," p. 99

> There are many possible sources of error in the performance appraisal process. One of the major sources is mistakes made by the rater. Although completely eliminating these errors is impossible, making raters aware of them through training is helpful.
> —Mathis and Jackson, *Human Resource Management*, p. 359

> Performance appraisals are diametrically in contradiction to the principles of quality management and the positive work environment that will be required for this new century.
> —Coens, "Say Goodbye to Performance Appraisals," p. 1

> When an impartial observer looks at the way most evaluations are conducted, he or she has to conclude that they are biased and unfair.
> —Robinson, *How to Conduct Employee Performance Appraisals*, p. A-2

Also, W. Edwards Deming is said to have exclaimed that appraisals were "the most powerful inhibitor to quality and productivity in the Western world." (Kohn, 1993, 129) After the many shortcomings of traditional performance appraisal systems are exposed, an innovative approach to performance management—the Performance Conversations® model—is introduced. The

Performance Conversations® model was designed with enlightened ideas, assumptions, and goals about performance and supervision. It restores value to the process of managers and subordinates working together to produce positive work outcomes.

Fundamental Flaws

The performance appraisal process has always had a number of critics. Even its supporters do not provide sufficient advice to overcome the inherent flaws that they readily admit.

Here are examples of flawed, appraisal-based thinking:

- feedback and appraisal are the same activity.

- supervisors are omniscient; they see and know all.

- all important indicators of performance are assessed on the appraisal instrument.

- people will respond to incentives the same way, every time.

- using appraisals is a fair way of making pay decisions.

Appraisals inspire hatred and distrust among employees who are the recipients of appraisals because they are seldom applied consistently across organizations. The problems with their use are so omnipresent that they are transparent. Organizations assume that they are valuable and, without understanding, continue blindly conducting evaluations. It would be far wiser to abandon the tool and create a different system free from the encumbrances associated with this tainted process.

> The hardest practices to change are those we take for granted. It's the things that "everybody knows" that get us in biggest trouble. What we know for sure stands in the way of what we need to learn, and keeps us managing with outmoded tools.
>
> —Farson and Keyes, *The Innovation Paradox*, p. xii

The varied answers to the basic question of why we use appraisals are surprising. We will uncover the real purposes of appraisal and offer alternative solutions to meet the needs of organizations.

We will uncover the real purposes of appraisal and offer alternative solutions to meeting the needs of organizations.

Why Continue to Repair a Broken System?

The very premise of appraising performance is challenged by the fifteen falla-cies of performance appraisals presented in this book. Even if only a handful of the problems with appraisals were acknowledged, that would provide sufficient justification to abandon their use. The system is fundamentally flawed at the core of its architecture. Why attempt to repair a broken system?

The problems with performance appraisals are widely documented in man-agement-related books. The sheer volume of problems, the negative impact associated with the use of appraisals, and the questionable nature of their accu-racy should indicate to managers that something is terribly wrong. It is actually amazing that organizations still use them and defend their use. The Perfor-mance Conversations® model is an alternative to appraisals.

Performance Appraisals are Theory X Management

It appears as if management science has ignored important research and argu-ments against the use of performance appraisal. A major criticism of appraisals is that they are built upon Theory X management.

> Theory X assumes that people hate work, are not ambitious, are not respon-sible, and prefer to be told what to do. Theory X managers believe people work only as long as they are watched, must be told specifically what to do, and how to do it, and must be closely controlled until they do it. Theory Y managers, on the other hand, push authority down, assuming employees have a natural interest and willingness to work and do well at their jobs. These managers seek out ideas from their employees, looking for better ways of doing things.
>
> —McKirchy, *How to Conduct Win-Win Performance Appraisals*, p. 46

Theory X thinking results in paternalistic and controlling systems because it assumes that employees are not trustworthy. In contrast, Theory Y manage-ment assumes that people inherently seek to do well. Ken Blanchard, coau-thor of the *One Minute Manager,* stated in Bob Nelson's *1001 Ways to Reward Employees*, "No employee seeks to be mediocre; all seek to be magnificent." (Nelson, 1994, ix) Advanced human resources approaches, such as empower-ment, self-directed work teams, participatory management, and quality circles, acknowledge the Theory Y viewpoint. Performance appraisals represent the state of the art personnel management thinking of the mid-1900s, and that is definitely Theory X thinking.

A Rotten Egg by Any Other Name Will Still Smell Foul

Appraisal, assessment, review, and evaluation are terms often used to describe the process of managing employee performance. Regardless of the term used, the desired result in each of these systems is better work performance. Each label appears to describe a particular perspective of performance, and each label is a telling descriptor of the psychological basis for gauging employee performance. The designs of the tools used follow this same logic.

- Appraisal implies the formulation of a judgment or conclusion, with some connotation of financial value.

- Evaluation denotes an assessment of worth (in financial and non-financial terms) and quality, and it explicitly implies a focus on the past.

- Review also accurately describes an exercise that looks backwards in time.

- Performance management is a term that is generally accepted to mean all activities that are related to designing, planning, managing, and appraising performance.

Performance management also encompasses the use of individual development plans, goal setting, and other forward-looking activities.

With this line of reasoning, the name Performance Conversations® also implies its orientation. The Performance Conversations® model is built upon ongoing problem-solving dialogue between managers and subordinates. The intentional emphasis is on *conversations* instead of evaluations.

The term *performance management* is used to describe both traditional and more advanced approaches to monitoring and regulating individual efforts. In this book, *performance management* is used only for illustrative purposes, as there is no other obvious term that would help us better communicate about the subject. The term will be used most often to describe alternative and proposed models for better management of people as there does not appear to be a more descriptive phrase that does not carry the same negative connotation as "appraisal."

The Performance Conversations® model is
built upon ongoing problem-solving dialogue between
managers and subordinates. The intentional emphasis is on
conversations instead of evaluations.

A Major Shift

Advancing our thinking, understanding, and performance management practice requires a major shift in perspective. This is not possible by incremental movement, but only by a radical departure from twentieth-century approaches. In this book, therefore, assertive language and disturbingly obvious logic will be used without discretion.

This book will validate what many have always known intuitively; our emotional and gut level reactions to performance appraisal signal something that should be questioned. Innate discomfort and fear of performance appraisals are well founded. We sense something is wrong with appraisals, and we are right to have such fervent reactions.

The leadership and management of employees are not rocket science. Some managers do it intuitively and do it well; the rest of us must go to business schools to learn ways to get it wrong!

A back-to-basics approach will be advocated throughout the book. The most basic approach is to treat employees with respect and as partners.

Fallacies, Truths, Solutions, and the Model

The fifteen most significant challenges associated with appraisals are detailed in Part II. Evidence to refute the prevailing thoughts about each of these problems is presented along with advice to avoid them. The collective solutions of these fifteen fallacies of appraisal were used to design an ideal model—the Performance Conversations® model.

Wake-Up Call

The first step toward improvement is acknowledging that there is a problem. Everyone interviewed in the process of developing this book admitted that there are numerous serious flaws with many elements of performance appraisal. Few interviewed were initially willing to outright disown the use of appraisals, but all provided excellent examples of past appraisal failures, which I will share. Upon thoughtful reflection, and when offered an alternative, the skeptics became advocates of an alternative approach. We must face reality and admit that performance appraisals have never worked successfully. This book is an alarm clock or bucket of cold water for those still entranced by the idea of successful performance appraisals.

Performance appraisals are classic twentieth-century
thinking built for an industrial world.

Appraisals—An Outdated Idea

Performance appraisals are classic twentieth-century thinking built for an industrial world. When appraisals were created, we did not have current ideas in our management vocabulary. Instead, we talked about behaviorism, Skinner boxes, sticks and carrots, negative reinforcement, boss and employee, control, and machine models of productivity. Our language was entrenched in Theory X management.

The vocabulary of today's leaders includes empowerment, engagement, employee involvement, knowledge management, job enrichment, coaching, quality circles, and Total Quality Management (TQM). These phrases are all reflective of Theory Y management. In an information economy built upon intellectual capital, we need a new model for performance management and a new language to better communicate.

An Alternative Approach

The good news is that if we change some of our assumptions, adjust our frame of reference, and utilize a few proven techniques, the shortcomings of appraisal can be avoided. The Performance Conversations® model combines the collective solutions from a number of successful supervision techniques with proven feedback strategies and advances in management science. This creates a system that uses the very best of twenty-first-century approaches to people management.

Quick Reference Points

Chapter 1

- Appraisals do not work.

- All the experts agree that appraisals have significant limitations and shortcomings.

- Avoiding appraisal systems is better than trying to fix them.

- Appraisals are an outdated idea built for the twentieth century.

- Appraisals are Theory X management at its worst.

- There will be fifteen fallacies of appraisals discussed in this book.

- The Performance Conversations® model is a twenty-first-century alternative to appraisals.

CHAPTER 2

The Performance Conversations®
Model—An Overview

The magic comes when two people communicate, break through their
problems and obstacles, celebrate their success, and plan for more.

—K. McKirchy

Can We Talk? Communication and Conversations

PEOPLE GET ALONG WELL and work well together if they are in constant communication with one another. In any human endeavor where there exists a
problem between individuals or groups of people, the solution to resolving
the difficulty is through full, open, and honest communication. Whether it is
counseling, mediation, diplomacy, negotiation, or conciliation, the basic method to resolution is via a two-way exchange of information and perspective.

The skillful use of the art of conversation has many and varied business applications. The Performance Conversations® model is built upon this universal
idea. Most traditional appraisals rely on the supervisor's assessment of performance alone, and wholeheartedly discourage or even suppress the employee's
communication. Essentially, they expect the employee to only verbally indicate
that they agree or accept the supervisor's assessment. If the employee gives any
other response, it is often called a "rebuttal." The model for most performance
appraisal systems is much more akin to monologues than dialogue. Conversations are important to problem solving at work and are fundamental ingredients in performance management.

In any human endeavor where there exists a
problem or crisis between individuals or groups
of people, the solution to resolving the difficulty
is through full, open, and honest communication.

The Model

The Performance Conversations® model of performance management has several major features:

Feature	Use
Future oriented	Aimed at improving performance, instead of documenting the past.
Non-evaluative	Does not rate performance, instead describes, analyzes, and interprets it.
Feedback based	Supervisor gives *and* receives information that is used to improve performance.
Dialogue driven	Conversational, non-judgmental, two-way exchange of information.
Collaborative	Partnership between employee and manager.
Operational	Aimed at problem solving and troubleshooting performance.
Investigative	Emphasizes data gathering and record keeping.
Continuous	Frequent meetings designed to seek clarity and understanding about desired performance.
Multidimensional	Tracks efforts, behaviors, and outcomes.
Corrective	Dedicated to making continuous adjustments to calibrate and recalibrate efforts.
Integrative	Supervision and performance management are combined

The Performance Conversations® model is a structured feedback and supervision system that uses continuous dialogue and adjustments to manage work efforts, outcomes, and behaviors.

In this model, the employee is an equal partner in the process of planning, managing, and monitoring performance. The employee is an active participant, giving and receiving feedback to and from the supervisor. Co-performance is fundamental to the Performance Conversations® process; the manager co-owns the employee's performance.

This model focuses on collecting performance data. Both the supervisor and the employee gather data about the employee's efforts, behaviors, and results, and then they meet regularly to discuss and analyze the information. The manager and employee seek agreement on what the performance data means and on the actions to be taken. This process is very verbal by nature and assumes that the path to a solution is through discussion and cooperation. The employee helps to identify and eliminate performance challenges. The employee and manager collaborate on their performance.

> Both the supervisor and the employee gather data about the employee's efforts, behaviors, and results, and then they meet periodically to discuss and analyze the information.

Their assessment of performance is never conclusive; it is ongoing. Continuous adjustments are made to refine performance. Time is not spent trying to rate the performance, but rather describing, analyzing, and interpreting it. Then plans are made to adjust, correct, or replicate it. It is positive trial and error, continuous quality improvement. Once optimal performance is reached, dialogue and adjustments continue in order to maintain successful outcomes.

> The employee helps to identify and eliminate performance challenges. The employee and manager collaborate on their performance.

Performance Conversations® are Operational

Performance Conversations® are not day-to-day conversations about the weather and the grandkids. Performance Conversations® are:

- about what we are doing today that advances our work-related goals.

- about efforts, activities, outcomes, and, ultimately, results.

- a structure used to calibrate and recalibrate the joint efforts of subordinates and supervisors.

- operational and seek to diagnose problems, brainstorm options, and plan for optimum performance.

These conversations acknowledge efforts, recognize contributions, and celebrate successes. The dialogue is critical and reflective, involves discovery and analysis, and is based upon the information provided by both the employee and the manager regarding their work. Performance Conversations® create the structured opportunity to step back from what is happening to understand what is going on at a macro level. While informative, these conversations can, and should be, free-flowing and informal, as appropriate.

Performance Conversations® encourage free-flowing, two-way dialogue about all factors related to the work tasks.

Performance Conversations®, Not Performance Counseling

Performance Conversations® encourage free-flowing, two-way dialogue about all factors related to the work tasks. It is not a manager being critical of an employee. It is not an omniscient supervisor dispensing justice to an employee that is not fully capable of understanding his own work. Nor is it the employee bringing a problem, dropping it on the manager's lap, and waiting for the manager to solve it. Performance Conversations® involve two people working together to create the best possible conditions for great performance. They embody the question, "What are *we* going to do to improve?"

Performance Conversations® involve two people working together to create the best possible conditions for great performance. They embody the question, "What are *we* going to do to improve?"

Performance Conversations® do not have the goal of rating performance or laying blame for performance that is not optimal. Instead, they focus upon creating an environment that produces ideal performance and removes obstacles to attaining it. When employees are involved in troubleshooting, problem solving, and diagnosis, they are far more likely to help generate solutions that prevent performance problems from reoccurring. Solutions generated by employees are more likely to be effective than solutions that were simply given to employees to execute.

If management removes the fear of retaliation, employees are encouraged to get engaged in problem resolution.

If management removes the fear of retaliation, employees are encouraged to get engaged in problem resolution. Since Performance Conversations® are not a means of rating, they can create an air of collaboration instead of the

"Anything you say can and will be used against you" perspective found in many Performance Review discussions.

Performance Conversations® do not have the goal of rating performance or laying blame for performance that is not optimal.

Communication, Cooperation, and Collaboration

The Performance Conversations® model focuses on communication, cooperation, and collaboration.

The Performance Conversations® model focuses on communication, cooperation, and collaboration. These ideas embody three of the principles discussed throughout the book, dialogue, employee involvement, and partnership. Dialogue is indicative of feedback and information exchange. Cooperation and employee involvement reinforce the requirement that employees be involved in each phase of performance, from planning and implementation to monitoring and assessment. Collaboration is a key component of partnerships when supervisors and subordinates agree on the terms of their co-performance.

Performance Conversations® and Performance Improvement

Performance Conversations® focus on quality control and performance improvement.

Performance Conversations® focus on quality control and performance improvement. The conversations create multiple opportunities to problem solve and agree on solutions. This process addresses difficult subject matter directly. It provides a safe place to confront tough issues while they are small; this reduces the gap between planned and actual performance. It is also an opportunity to recognize good performance and plan for future performance. It provides continuous movement towards the ideal, and each conversation is equivalent to calibrating or recalibrating efforts.

One of the greatest advantages of this model is that problems are dealt with frequently and timely. At a planned interval, typically every four to ten weeks, there is a structured opportunity to deal with problems and make corrections and adjustments. Smaller adjustments are easier to make than large ones. Frequency facilitates ease of change and reduces the toxicity of any negative feedback. The angle theory of feedback discussed later in this chapter is the best example of this approach.

Conversations and Feedback

> If we are going to successfully manage performance, we need to *discuss* what has been done well and what needs improvement. The employee needs to learn from both positive and negative feedback and collaborate in plans to improve performance and build upon successes.
>
> —Tetreault, Letter to the author, p. 2

It has been said that "feedback is the breakfast of champions" (Blanchard and Lober, 1984, 66). Daily or frequent conversations about work tasks facilitate more meaningful conversations about work in general. When large challenges are presented, the environment of dialogue (and hopefully trust) is already established, which should make it easier to discuss and deal with these issues as they occur. Informal conversations that occur over time are a necessary part of the formal performance management process. While informal, Performance Conversations® are planned opportunities to share information and engage in two-way, open, and honest exchange.

> Discussing the little things that need to be addressed as they occur reduces the possibility that big things will happen.

The Angle Theory of Feedback

> It will be "employee friendly" if it provides sufficient objective feedback with adequate timeliness so that if there is a problem, it can be corrected before it is repeated.
>
> —Laurel, *Performance Appraisal*, p. 4

The angle theory of feedback describes the gap between desired performance and actual performance in relation to a function of time. The assumption is that the supervisor and subordinate start off at the same point, but due to lack of clarity, training, proper effort, or coordination about what is expected or needed, their paths begin to diverge quickly. The longer the time between when a problem occurs and when the employee and the supervisor intervene, the greater the disparity (gap) will be between expected and actual outcomes.

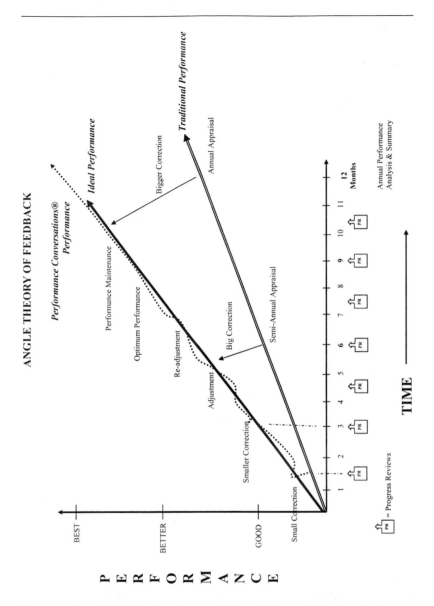

ANGLE THEORY OF FEEDBACK

Over time, traditional and ideal performance grows further and further apart unless there is an intervention. The Performance Conversations® approach gives supervisors multiple structured opportunities to adjust performance through the use of frequent feedback sessions (Progress Reviews) over the reporting period. These occasions ensure that employee performance is in line with expections and that corrections are made when small.

The sooner the supervisor intervenes, the better. If a correction occurs quickly, it is more likely to be a small adjustment that is easy to make, and the adjustment is more likely to be successful. This theory of feedback acknowledges the need for timely feedback and interaction between managers and employees. "The time to correct an employee's mistake is when it happens. Don't allow an error to become a habit" (McKirchy, 1994, p. 11).

Continual feedback is basic to increased productivity and successful partnerships. But as conditions change, feedback is also necessary to sustain good performance. Dialogue and cooperation create the opportunity to align and adjust performance around a desired constant level of acceptability.

> The sooner the supervisor intervenes, the better. If a correction occurs quickly, it is more likely to be a small adjustment that is easy to make, and the adjustment is more likely to be successful.

One Correction Does Not Equal Success

It is usually not possible to change poor performance with one single correction or conversation. Human behavior does not respond like a machine with an on-and-off-switch. The more probable scenario will involve multiple conversations and interventions to move human behavior toward a newer but more desirable equilibrium. Aristotle noted, "We are what we repeatedly do. Excellence, then, is not an act but a habit." Managers and employees meet to discuss work tasks and determine ways to adjust their efforts; they repeat this cycle as necessary, indefinitely.

> It is usually not possible to change poor performance with one single correction or conversation.

Negative Feedback Is Toxic, But Palatable in Small Doses

One advantage of early intervention is that the correction offered is less dramatic. Similar to getting treatment for a serious illness before it spreads throughout the body, early intervention is always positive. Continuing the medical analogy, smaller doses of a toxic medicine over a long period of time may treat a condition, wherein one large dose would be fatal.

Some managers use what social scientists have termed the "wait and zap" method of performance management. Managers accumulate a year's worth of criticism, and give the employee one big dose of it at the annual performance evaluation. This approach may be catastrophic for some employees. Employees may leave (or be terminated) upon finding out that they have been unaware of poor performance for ten months.

Negative feedback is unavoidable, yet it can be a positive element in helping employees grow and improve. Supervisors can manage the dosage of such feedback by giving negative (and positive) feedback as close to the performance event as possible. Frequent feedback will cause constant alignment versus more dramatic adjustments. Using Progress Reviews in the Performance Conversations® method is an ideal way to provide both positive and negative feedback.

Data Collection Is Better Than "Documentation"

Data collection differs from "documentation" in its intent and purpose. Data collection tracks efforts, activities, behaviors, and results for the purpose of analyzing, describing, monitoring, and managing performance. Documentation is keeping track of mistakes, performance failures, bad behavior, and other negative events. Documentation is one dimensional, directional (toward justifying a decision that is often already made). It is also limited in time—commonly the time when the employee is "under the gun."

Data collection is far better than documentation, for it is evidence of good, poor, and neutral performance over time. It is better than negative documentation, in that it provides an early warning system that alerts the supervisor to the occasion when the employee starts performing poorly. If data collection is conducted on an ongoing basis, it will contain many important indicators of all performance.

Data collection tracks efforts, activities, behaviors, and results for the purpose of analyzing, describing, monitoring, and managing performance. Documentation is keeping track of mistakes, performance failures, bad behavior, and other negative examples.

If both the supervisor and employee are actively engaged in data collection as a quality control measure, there is no need for the supervisor to create additional "documentation" that would justify an employee's potential termination. The evidence will be transparent and openly available to the supervisor and the employee. If the employee is involved in data collection and data analysis, the performance level will be all too obvious. Data will be available at the earliest possible time, early enough for the employee to take action to correct the poor performance.

Data collection is also more impartial than documentation, as it is gathered on all employees regardless of whether they are performing well, average, or poorly. It negates any accusations of biased or preferential supervisory behavior. Data collection makes "documentation" obsolete.

Supervision and Performance Management

One of the key principles of the Performance Conversations® model is that good supervision is good performance management. Therefore, poor supervision is nearly catastrophic to good performance management. There is no circumstance in which an expert model of performance management can exist if the supervisor administering it does not manage day-to-day performance well.

A worse scenario is if the manager engages in disrespectful and belittling behavior or just relates poorly with subordinates. Therefore, a great deal of time should be spent on creating the environment or culture in which performance occurs. A complement to the right work environment is the relationship between the individual and the manager. A poor relationship will inhibit performance, just as a good relationship will fuel it.

Relationships and Performance

An organization is only as good as its managers. Relationships between managers and subordinates do not have to be personal or intimate, but they most certainly must be genuine, cordial, and respectful. A trusting relationship is also essential to a productive relationship. It is through the manager that the employee perceives the organization. This is consistent with the popular human resources saying that "People do not quit organizations, they quit managers."

An Organization Is Only as Good as Its Managers

Conversations, Not Evaluations

Conversations are communication; evaluations are judgments. In order to improve performance, the individual and the manager must talk. Ideal performance must be described, the obstacles to ideal performance must be identified, and performance action plans must be agreed upon. Evaluating performance on appraisal instruments is not a necessary ingredient to good performance. Evaluations are reflective, retrospective judgments about the past. Passing judgment often creates emotional and irrational responses. Evaluations can be punitive, are almost always subjective, and are most often counterproductive.

Constructive criticism is seldom received in the manner in which it was intended. Formal appraisals often miss their intended aims because the improvement message gets lost in the criticism offered. Timely, information-based feedback (without laying blame or passing judgment) that is discussed openly between employee and supervisor is a superior management approach to appraisal.

People Management Is an Investment

No deposit, no return. Performance cannot be managed twice a year with a form designed by the human resources department, because performance occurs daily. Elements of any good performance management system must be fully integrated with supervision—performance and supervision are inextricably tied to one another. Managers that are too busy to track their staff's performance are too busy to care for the organization's greatest investment—the employees. The fact is that they are too busy to be effective supervisors. After all, supervision involves supervising—that is, facilitating and monitoring the execution of the organization's work products.

When employees are improperly supervised, their results are less than optimal. It is no wonder that many employees are surprised at the end of the reporting period to learn that their efforts were not up to par. They were never told. The supervisor is then in the unenviable position of communicating bad news at the annual performance evaluation review. The primary role of the supervisor is to help individuals perform better than they would alone. If the supervisor does not accomplish better performance, there is no value added, and supervision becomes unnecessary overhead.

To effectively manage performance is an investment of time and effort. If all employees did what they were instructed to do, each time without direction, then many supervisory and managerial positions would be unnecessary. Coaching and support are critical to individual success. Thus, there will always be a need for good supervisors; but supervision is an active, ongoing, and detailed responsibility.

Supervision and performance management are two sides of the same coin. Fortunately, the Performance Conversations® model accounts for, and gives tools to facilitate, good supervision—it is built into the model.

Performance Management Is Not An Administrative Activity

One of the myths that HR people have helped to perpetuate is that the performance management process is simply an administrative task required by HR or senior management. Appraisals are most often used to make decisions about pay, promotions, layoffs, and other personnel matters. Many managers and employees see the process only as a necessary evil to satisfy external organizational requirements. Yet, the primary purposes of performance management are to sustain good performance, correct poor performance, and improve performance, all of which are specific to the activity between the manager and employee.

How Do You Know Your Employees Are Doing Well? Prove it!

If you ask the average supervisor for documentation that justifies a termination, it is likely that you will get thorough documentation. If you ask that same supervisor for evidence of good performance, he or she will likely say, "I just know the employee is performing well." There should be equal evidence of both good performance and poor performance.

Most supervisors do not do a good job of tracking performance on a day-to-day or week-to-week basis; instead, they rely on performance summaries that are commonly several months or even years old. Since solid supervision is the basic building block to good performance management, any system for performance management must be fully integrated with the task of supervision. Performance evidence should be balanced—good, bad, or neutral. This allows proper diagnosis of performance to determine what to encourage, what to change, and what needs improvement.

Performance Dimensions

An ideal performance management system accounts for all the dimensions of performance, fully integrates with basic supervision, and appropriately documents all the indicators of performance. Many traditional systems are flawed because only outcomes are tracked. However, bad behavior can mar good performance; individuals might try very hard but still fail. Performance is dynamic and multidimensional, and its spectrum cannot be reduced to a single instrument with seven performance dimensions. Even those systems that are designed by supposed experts are flawed if they assume that a single static paper form will track, measure, and account for all dimensions of performance. Performance appraisal systems designed with twentieth-century performance assumptions are ill-equipped to handle employment relationships that are built upon such contemporary approaches as empowerment and employee involvement.

Unless the performance-management system used gives the employee enough information about improvement points and proper support to change them, it is doubtful the performance management system will improve performance.

The Future Is Now

Appraisals look backwards, but performance is prospective. The goals of performance management systems should be to correct poor performance, replicate good performance, and improve all performance. Yet, most appraisal systems mistakenly focus their attention on the past by emphasizing the rating of past performance during the annual performance-review ritual. These ratings become an end unto themselves, rather than a way to help create and sustain performance over time. Improved performance will occur only through proper coaching, guidance, training, and employee support. Unless the performance-management system used gives the employee enough information about improvement points and proper support to change them, it is doubtful the performance management system will improve performance. The requirement for improved performance is open and honest dialogue—performance conversations.

> The goals of performance management systems should be to correct poor performance, replicate good performance, and improve all performance.

The Building Blocks

The key ideas presented in the aforementioned paragraphs are building blocks for the Performance Conversations® model. They are summarized as follows:

- **Good Supervision** – a prerequisite for good performance management

- **Employee Involvement** – in the planning, tracking, and monitoring of work

- **Two-way Feedback** – between manager and employee

- **Conversations** – ongoing problem-solving dialogue

- **Not Evaluations** – description and diagnosis emphasized, instead of judgment

- **Partnership** – jointly identified and agreed upon problems, solutions, and action plans

- **Data Collection** – evidence gathered to show progress on goals and plans

- **Efforts, Behaviors, and Outcomes** – are all accounted for in managing performance

- **Future Oriented** – emphasis on performance improvement, not rating past efforts

- **Relationships** – built through coaching and support

Each of these ideas help to redefine how managers and employees work together and share responsibility for common goals. They are characteristic of a more progressive approach to supervision in the twenty-first century.

The Performance Conversations® Model – By Definition

The Performance Conversations® model is designed to overcome the limitations and shortcomings of traditional appraisals. The effectiveness of Performance Conversations® is the integration of solutions from several successful performance management and supervision techniques. By definition, the Performance Conversations® model is a structured feedback and supervision system that uses continuous dialogue and adjustments to manage work efforts, outcomes, and behaviors. Don't worry; all of this will be explained in a simple, straightforward manner later.

The Performance Conversations® model is a simple concept. It is so elegantly simple to grasp and understand that even top management will be able to use it. One of the greatest advantages of the model is that the employee actually does fifty percent of the work. The employee becomes the first step in the quality assurance process. The employee will learn to track and document his own work efforts and outcomes—employee involvement at is best. The employee rightfully becomes a partner in the process of managing and regulating performance.

Steps in the Right Direction

There are five steps in the Performance Conversations® model. Each was designed to incorporate the considerations noted above and to avoid the common challenges associated with traditional appraisals. Combined, the steps create numerous structured and planned opportunities for managers and employees to meet to discuss operational and work-related matters. Through this guided and sustained dialogue, ideal performance outcomes not only become attainable, but routine.

1. **Performance Plans:** In the spirit of partnership, the employee is involved in the development of a strategy to coordinate their efforts with their manager's.

2. **Performance Logs:** The employee and manager track their joint efforts, outcomes, and behaviors in individual logs which are used to describe what is happening, when, and how it happens.

3. **Performance Portfolios:** Documents are gathered to validate that their actions and activities are producing the right results.

4. **Progress Reviews:** Periodic conversations are held to discuss the contents of the Performance Logs and Performance Portfolio and to make adjustments based upon this information.

5. **Annual Performance Analysis and Summary (APAS):** An annual discussion is held to discern patterns and trends, to celebrate successes, and to use the year's information to create future successes.

The richness of communication comes from the fact that the conversations are about the evidence of performance that both parties have collected. The frequency of conversation ensures that efforts are coordinated, that activities are monitored, and that outcomes are tracked. Their discussions are focused on ways to meet their shared goals and shared responsibilities. Performance Conversations® is a system of feedback that ensures the right work-related information is shared in a timely fashion in order to create and recreate the best performance results.

Old School Critics

Some will argue that it is un-American not to have a system based upon competition and numerical ranking. Managers that are old school and firm but fair might even argue that the new model is soft. If it is soft, it is because it does not give a paternalistic upper hand to the manager in case "that pesky employee does not do what he is told." So, in addition to introducing the Performance Conversations® model, this book thoroughly critiques traditional appraisal systems and refutes the ideas upon which they are built.

By the time enlightened managers reach Chapter 10, you will have long abandoned the idea that appraisals are a wise method of managing performance. You will also know why using any appraisal technique will ultimately fail. By that time, you will be hungry for a better approach to managing people in the twenty-first century. Using the Performance Conversations® model will be appreciated best after the limitations and fallacies of traditional appraisals have been exposed.

The Road Ahead

A major advantage of the Performance Conversations® approach is that it makes supervision and performance management seamless. Managers need not use a particular supervision technique and then create a separate annual or semi-annual process to track and record performance; in the Performance Conversations® approach they are part and parcel of one another. Chapter 3 explains why supervision is the most important element in performance management and without proper supervision, all performance management efforts fail. Chapters 4 to 7 detail why each step in the Performance Conversations® model is useful in negating the Fallacies of Performance Appraisal and how their use will create a better performance management system.

Quick Reference Points

Chapter 2

- All human problems are solved through active communication.

- Problem-solving conversations are superior to written evaluations.

- A good performance management system integrates with supervision.

- Performance Conversations® are operational, work-related discussions.

- The model is future oriented and non-evaluative.

- The employee and supervisor have multiple opportunities to talk and solve problems.

- They both gather performance data.

- They meet frequently to calibrate and recalibrate their joint efforts; they co-perform.

- They share information, give one another feedback, and negotiate options.

- They agree upon options, and put them into play.

- They communicate, cooperate, and collaborate.

- The name of the game is feedback; the sooner it is shared, the better it is.

- They hold an annual Performance Planning meeting.

- They each maintain a Performance Log to record important performance information.

- They create a folder—Performance Portfolio—to hold all the evidence of performance that they have gathered.

- Frequent Progress Reviews are held to discuss the contents of their Performance Portfolio and Performance Log, and to address problems, reinforce good efforts, and give recognition.

- At the end of the year, they study the evidence of performance gathered and discussed over the year to uncover positive or negative trends. The results are used to plan for the next year.

- The Performance Conversations® model is a twenty-first-century approach to management.

Supervision and Performance Management

The Lowest Common Denominator for Performance Management

SUPERVISION IS THE LOWEST common denominator in performance management. Poor supervision is poor performance management. Poor supervision may not prevent good performance, but certainly suppresses it. Likewise, good supervision increases the likelihood of creating and regenerating good performance.

Good supervision is difficult and complex. Everything that happens at work can bear upon performance. The supervisor has to collect disparate sources of information, synthesize them daily, make decisions based upon this information, communicate the decisions to others, check the progress of plans, and then make appropriate adjustments.

This chapter on supervision helps to define and redefine management in the twenty-first century in such a way that it supports the ultimate goal of improving performance. Instead of spending tens of thousands of dollars and many months customizing a performance management system, organizations would be better served spending an equivalent amount of time and resources developing the supervision skills of managers.

> Supervision is the lowest common denominator
> in performance management.

Supervision = Performance Management

One of the most important messages that this chapter reinforces is that supervision and performance management are identical tasks. One of the mistaken ideas that HR professionals have helped to convey to managers over the past fifty years is that performance appraisal is an additional administrative activity that is added onto their supervisory responsibilities. Nothing could be further from the truth. The planning, tracking, accounting for, and managing of employee performance is the most basic of supervisory duties.

The Performance Conversations® model reintegrates performance management back into the normal activities of supervisors. As a matter of fact, it provides managers with a successful framework for managing day-to-day performance so that supervision and performance management are not only inseparable, but virtually identical. Thus, the manager's daily duties become indistinguishable from performance management responsibilities.

Feedback Is Performance Management

> Feedback is much more than sharing performance information. Feedback can build a relationship between you and your staff in which you can learn to count on each other. Having the courage to tell the truth and ask for it in return increases trust and our ability to work together.
>
> —Maurer, *The Feedback Toolkit*, p. 20

Employees want feedback, but not appraisal. Giving feedback is necessary and effective. Frequent informal conversations about work can be as effective as any formal evaluation system. The frequent interaction creates the opportunity to solve performance challenges as they occur and before the situation worsens.

All activities that an employee and manager do together are indicators of what is important and necessary. These indicators should be shared openly. In fact, employees should also help gather information about their work. Even if managers were to share only information they have collected, this would likely be *enough* information to positively affect performance and reduce the need for a formal performance management system. An employee presented with enough information that *accurately* shows the results of his efforts will likely respond to this information in a way that will help good performance to continue or to correct poor performance. Emphasis should be placed on *enough* and *accurate,* because sparse or summarized information that does not describe the full measure of performance may rightfully produce resentful, negative reactions from the employee.

Frequent informal conversations about work can be as effective
as any formal evaluation system.

Managers Want (and Need) Feedback

> The best managers find ways to get feedback from their staff. This is a bit sur-
> prising since most organizational structures emphasize top-down feedback
> and offer no formal way for a boss to receive it. These people have to *work* at
> getting the feedback they need.
>
> —Maurer, *The Feedback Toolkit*, p. 8

Managers must receive feedback from their employees to understand how they are aiding or hindering their subordinates' work. One important supervisory responsibility is to remove obstacles to good performance. The manager must actively solicit feedback from subordinates, recognize the value of subordinate feedback, and take action on perceived weaknesses.

Prior to the exchange of feedback, the manager must have created an environment wherein the subordinate feels comfortable and free from retaliation to give honest feedback. The employee must also feel that giving feedback is a requirement. All human relationships are built upon the premise of honest and effective communication.

Telling Isn't Teaching or Managing

Two old adages from education are that *telling isn't teaching* and *teaching is not learning*. A teacher who lectures in the front of the room and assumes that all students have learned the material equally well is a relic of the twentieth century. All available educational evidence tells us that the lecture method of instruction is the least effective form of teaching, even while schools and colleges are filled with lecturers. A similar problem exists within organizations with dinosaur-like supervisors.

Supervisors who tell employees how to do something once and expect it to done the way they want it done, the first time, and to their degree of satisfaction, are mistaken. If this were possible, there would be far fewer managers and supervisors in the world.

Despite educational research that shows people are either auditory (tell me), visual (show me), kinesthetic (let me do it), or some combination of the three, most classrooms rely only on the "tell me" method of instruction, the lecture. Yet, classroom instruction, training, and supervision often rely upon the "I told you to do it this way" method of communicating how things should be done. Good supervision must include dialogue.

Good supervision would use the "tell me, show me, let me do it, let's talk about it, and repeat the cycle until we are both clear" method. It would also include the "checking back periodically to exchange information and feedback" method of working with others. Often these basic supervision techniques are not practiced, so performance management is made considerably more difficult.

What Managers Must Do to Be Successful

Managers must understand their organization, its culture, its policies and procedures, and its work systems. They must attempt to understand how everything at work affects their work and their subordinates' work. It is a tall order, so managers need help. The best source of assistance is their subordinates. Only with the help of subordinates will all indicators of performance be uncovered, analyzed, and synthesized.

Indicators

Everything that an employee and manager do surrounding work is an *indicator* of the quality and character of the individuals' contributions—their performance. It is a collection of activities, efforts, behaviors, results, accomplishments, failures, successes, and trials. Some actions are more notable than others. A series of small actions can be as important, or more important, than a single noteworthy effort. In short, everything is an indicator.

The Critical Incident method of performance appraisal may be a useful tool in managing performance, but it diminishes the value of small actions that may be of even greater importance. Many key performance indicators are lost in Performance Reviews because of their insignificance at the time they initially occur. Trends and patterns, by definition, develop over time and some seemingly insignificant factors may eventually become important. A collection of indicators may identify a critical trend.

Actions and behaviors that are large and small, periodic and continuous, and routine or special, should be accounted for in a good system of supervision and performance management. Some indicators are organizational indicators and some allude to the quality of supervision that employees receive. Indicators identified by subordinates will help to point out those structural and procedural factors that limit their performance on both a supervisory and organizational level.

Everything that an employee and manager do surrounding work is an *indicator* of the quality and character of the individuals' contributions—their performance.

Behaviors Are Also Indicators

Behaviors are also critical indicators of work and the character of work. An employee who is diligent but does not make the mark should be recognized for trying hard. The employee who performs well but is disrespectful to others should be reprimanded for hostile behavior. Employees who bypass official procedure to discover a better process should be recognized for initiative, but admonished for the procedure violation. How individuals work with others in the workplace is often as important as the performance of actual job duties. Supervision must manage behavior as it can spoil good performance or define it.

Efforts, Behavior, Results

A great effort can yield a poor result and vice versa. Management must be observant of the employee's great exertions that sometimes go unnoticed because they don't produce distinguished results. The motto of the Special Olympics captures this thought: "Let me win, but if I cannot win, let me be brave in the attempt." Let's reward also those brave employees that fall short of great results despite their struggle.

—Allender, "Reengineering Employee Performance Appraisals the TQM Way," p. 3

There is no substitute for good results. However, it would be prudent to understand the causes of poor results. Managers should note all efforts, as they are the building blocks upon which results are built. Performance management systems should account for efforts, behaviors, and results. These factors are inseparable. Each is an indicator of performance past, present, and future. Managers must learn to say "good try" for a subordinate's good effort, even if the outcome is not so highly regarded. Taking efforts, behaviors, and results into account is the equivalent to a balanced scorecard approach to individual contributions.

There is no substitute for good results. However, it would be prudent to understand the causes of poor results. Managers should note all efforts as they are the building blocks upon which results are built.

Documentation and Data Collection

It is a manager's responsibility to identify critical information that proves that work tasks are being executed successfully. What exactly should a supervisor track? Does the employee understand the expected outcomes? Do the supervisor and the employee agree on the indicators of successful performance, and can they prove to themselves, and others, that they are doing a good job?

Once these questions are answered, the evidence and indicators of performance gone well—or gone awry—can be collected and maintained for future analysis and historical purposes. Consistently gathered data that describes actual work as it occurs is all the documentation that is ever needed in performance management. Supervisors will have sufficient data accumulated to justify any personnel action, be it meritorious recognition or discipline. This same data will also provide the basis for performance improvement plans or elements that help reengineer work.

Documentation, Evidence, and Indicators

A manager that is diligent about performing her responsibilities is always looking for ways to validate performance. This validation is evidence. Managers should look for big indicators, small indicators, and medium-sized indicators, and look for trends by analyzing and synthesizing all information.

The indicators are documented in real time for analysis and interpretation later. Documents could include reports, summaries, letters, charts, results, thank-you letters, letters of reprimand, and warnings. Documents include all recorded information regarding the character and quality of work. The Performance Portfolio technique in the Performance Conversations® model was designed to be a repository of such information.

Evidence is often written, but may also include a finished product, a satisfied customer, a conflict resolved, an increase in sales, a change in behavior, a completed project, a completed model, or a computer program debugged. Evidence is always information that is observable, measurable, and verifiable. Evidence is anything that defines performance and validates whether or not desired performance was achieved.

Documentation, evidence, results, actions, and behaviors are all indicators. Performance is a complex matter and seldom is it able to be reduced to a single factor or fact. It is multidimensional, changing, ongoing, and flexible. Performance tends to occur in the many shades of gray. The Performance Conversations® model recognizes these factors and was designed to account for all the indicators of performance.

Documentation, evidence, results, actions, and behaviors are all indicators. Performance is a complex matter and seldom is it able to be reduced to a single factor or fact.

Performance Is Seldom Black and White

Performance is seldom black and white. Good effort with bad behaviors, success at too high a cost, satisfying customers only after they have complained, or finishing a project early but not following proper procedures are examples of performance elements that are both good and bad. A single decision or action can sometimes be the defining point of a good year or a less profitable year for an organization. Despite gallant efforts, a single thought, idea, or action can make a world of difference. A single action, however, should not diminish actions that came before or come after. A single action should always be viewed in full context. Remember, sometimes the action can be attributable to just plain luck!

Performance is almost always a matter of degree. If it were simply black or white, a person who could not or would not perform as expected would be quickly terminated. Performance management deals with gradients of performance. Performance is multidimensional and complex, therefore, every factor related to performance should be considered in performance discussions.

Useful Contemporary Models of Supervision

Situational Leadership

Every employee has a different capacity to contribute, given their readiness and willingness to approach their work. This is also affected by the individual task to be performed. A veteran employee who is learning a new task is not as able to perform at his normal high level. Appropriate adjustments by the supervisor are necessary to ensure that the employee is supervised based upon the circumstances. Paul Hershey's book on the subject, *The Situational Leader*, is an invaluable resource (1985), as is *Leadership and the One Minute Manager: Increasing Effectiveness through Situational Leadership* by Ken Blanchard and Patricia and Drea Zigarmi (1999). Good management is able to adapt to the specific individual, job task, and situation.

Supervising is directing, checking, controlling, and delivery.
Coaching is helping and supporting peak performance.

Coaching

Coaching is a technique for helping others reach peak performance and ultimate potential.

—Markle, *Catalytic Coaching*, p. 3

The coaching metaphor is certainly a better description of the role and relationship between a supervisor and subordinate in the twenty-first century than that of the traditional role of a *boss* and employee. Supervising is directing, checking, controlling, and delivery. Coaching is *helping* and *supporting* peak performance.

There are numerous resources available on the coaching approach to supervision. There are also several researchers who apply the idea of coaching to performance management, namely *Catalytic Coaching: The End of the Performance Review* by Garold L. Markle (2000).

Coaching generally has positive connotations while supervision generates fewer. The chart below summarizes some of the popular connotations associated with the two ideas:

COACHING	SUPERVISION
Helping	Monitoring
Supporting	Managing
Caring and concern	Watching
Working with	Working for
Developing	Training
Investing	Drawing-out
Inspiring	Motivating
Partnership	Authority
Mentoring	Supervising
Co-performance	Separate performances
Personal relationship	Work relationship

A coach's goal is to help individuals reach their full potential. Good coaches know that only through excellent individual performance will the team excel. They also know that the individual's performance is only good in the context of the rest of the team. The popular connotation of a boss is someone who requires the very best effort for the good of the organization; this perspective is closer to exploiting than of helping.

Coaches do not allow you to settle for less than your best. Coaches are known for yelling and screaming and demanding that you do not give up on yourself. Coaches believe in you. People frequently go back and visit their high school or college coaches. Not as many people go back to visit their old bosses or have fond memories of them. Coaching is about caring and concern for individuals—it builds relationships. Supervision is oversight on behalf of the organization, not for the individual; therefore, there is less of a lasting relationship.

Coaching is a better approach to working with others in the twenty-first century and represents a more enlightened approach to supervision.

Managers have fewer ways to influence employees and shape their behavior. Coercion is no longer an option; managers increasingly must serve as coaches to indirectly influence rather than demand desired behavior.

—Nelson, *1001 Ways to Reward Employees*, p. xi

Coaching helps to cultivate the idea of co-performance: the individual and their supervisor working together toward common ends—good performance.

Performance improvement can explode through a partnership with the employee.

Partnership

Performance improvement can explode through a partnership with the employee. Together the supervisor and employee diagnose performance anomalies, create plans to continue that which is going well, and correct that which needs their collective attention. The supervisor and employee are joined together working toward a common purpose; this is the true definition of teamwork. Since the employee and their supervisor co-perform, it is important that they understand that they are dependent upon one another for success. They are jointly responsible for outcomes and must create and manage a partnership.

Co-Performance and Responsible Employees

Twenty-first-century supervision is not possible if employees are allowed to shift the responsibility for performance management to the supervisor alone. In the traditional model of supervision, the employee simply comes to work and follows instructions without regard for the outcome or success of their efforts. These employees work by the clock, not by results or success. This situation will not produce lasting results because the employee has transferred the responsibility for results to the supervisor, who has less control of the outcome. The employee, not the supervisor, actually performs the work tasks. Employees and their managers co-perform like athletes and coaches. A better approach is the construct of co-performance, which requires the joint ownership of performance and outcomes (Bain, 2001).

The Language of Supervision

It can be argued that using the term coaching instead of supervision is just semantics or that performance appraisal and performance management is the same task. Others will say that feedback and evaluation are similar concepts, and any attempt to use politically correct words instead of traditional terms is just consultant-speak. The truth is the words we use to describe the world around us make a huge difference. Words reflect our perspectives, our belief systems, but more importantly, words direct our actions. With this in mind, we should examine our language and analyze what we communicate.

Much of management's common language is not conducive to positive relations with employees. Before we can change our thoughts about how we work with others, we need to change our rhetoric. Psychologists say that we must first change our knowledge and beliefs before we successfully change our actions. The information and thoughts about our language is just that important. As it will be discussed later, managers want to be coaches, not judges.

First, many managers use terms or phrases to describe employees that are not always positive. Language can reinforce power relationships and it can belittle employees. A popular southern phrase is to call nonexempt staff "good help." Managers sometimes describe subordinates as those who work "under me." This articulation of levels and use of *under* as if some people are "beneath" others is not always unintentional. Another typical phrase is to say that someone works *for* me. When in actuality they work *for* the company or organization and are not in servitude to the manager. Our language should be more accurate and respectful. Some better phrases are: *those I work with, my partners, teammates, colleagues,* or *associates.*

Second, some language that is typically used reinforces the stereotype that employees are not capable of being responsible or thinking. When someone works *for* you, it can imply that they do not work for themselves. They are not responsible for their efforts, only the supervisor is responsible. If we believe in the concept of co-performance, then the supervisor and employee form a partnership. Phrases such as, "What have we discovered about last week's production errors," instead of "You did not do what I asked you to do," is clearly more reflective of an enlightened perspective about relationships.

Third, there is an overemphasis on the word *they* when describing employees who are not a part of the management team. *They*, the employees, are often treated as an entire group of people who are somehow not connected to the rest of the organization. Terms such as *we, our partners, our team, our colleagues,* "*the people who actually make our products*" or "*those who serve our customers*" are better choices. The term *they* can perpetuate the myth that it is an "us against them" environment. It implies that somehow employees are not inextricably intertwined with the leaders of the organization, or that an adversarial relationship exists between leaders and employees.

Redefine Supervision

Initially, employees will be skeptical about the use of an alternative model of supervision because they have been trained to be reluctant, suspicious, and leery of managers. After all, managers are the enemy, they only want to get something out of me (labor), take something from me (performance) and will do something bad to me (punish), if I don't act (behave) as required. Therefore, before consideration of implementing a new approach to supervision, management should work to build a culture, climate, and work environment that is based upon fair treatment, trust, and partnerships. Once employees believe that the organization has their best interest at heart, they will be more likely to engage in a partnership with the organization and its managers. Until then, the manner in which supervisors relate to employees day-to-day will determine whether or not employees respond to the request for creating a new kind of relationship with their manager.

Conclusion

Employees and their managers should be partners working together toward a common goal—good performance outcomes. If the relationship is built upon an "us against them" or adversarial foundation, one side will attempt to achieve their goals at the expense of the other. Such perspectives will not produce sustained success. Traditional approaches to supervision must be reevaluated and redefined.

Good supervision starts with treating employees with respect, having frequent interaction, and involving employees in the planning, implementation, tracking, and assessment of their work. The work environment must be conducive to honesty, candor, and a two-way exchange of information. Giving and *receiving* feedback is a basic element of twenty-first-century management. Performance is an articulating process; it requires two-way interaction and communication. The manager must allow, expect, and take heed of feedback from the employee. How can they work "together" if communication and feedback flow in only one direction?

Quick Reference Points

Chapter 3

- Good supervision produces good performance outcomes.

- Supervision and performance management are the same activity.

- Feedback is the key.

- Everything that an employee does is an indicator of performance.

- Efforts, behaviors, results, and outcomes are all indicators.

- All indicators must be tracked in good management.

- Data collection is used to diagnose performance challenges.

- Coaching is the management approach of the future.

- Employees and their supervisors co-perform like an athlete and their coach.

- The language of supervision should emphasize employee engagement, partnership, shared goals, and shared responsibilities.

Part II

Common Challenges

Critics of performance appraisal present a number of compelling arguments against its use. Anecdotal, empirical, and personal experience demonstrates a multitude of problems with appraisal practices. The main critiques are that the individual performance appraisal assumes a false degree or measurement accuracy, engenders dysfunctional employee conflict and competition, assigns an inordinate amount of responsibility for poor performance to individual employees while undervaluing the importance of the overall work process, underemphasizes the importance of the work group, and is often used as a managerial 'Theory X' control device.

—Gary E. Roberts

The Performance Conversations® model was not designed to overcome the fallacies of appraisal but to avoid them altogether. Performance Appraisals are classic twentieth-century thinking built for an industrial world. In the twenty-first-century knowledge economy, human potential cannot be reduced to seven indices on an appraisal instrument. The appraisal model should be scrapped and a newer more innovative way to manage people must be considered.

Chapters 4-7 delineate the major shortcomings, false assumptions, and design flaws associated with traditional appraisals. The chapters also offer solutions to each of these common challenges. The solutions collectively form the foundation of the Performance Conversations® model.

Fallacies of Purpose

THE FALLACIES OF PURPOSE are the false reasons and context in which performance appraisals are currently used in most organizations. The fallacies highlight the mistaken beliefs about appraisals, the misdirected efforts in using them, and the misplaced emphasis on the past. Regardless of how well they are designed, or rigorously implemented and used, performance appraisals will not meet their intended purpose. Most performance management tools are designed and implemented utilizing some or all of these fallacies:

Fallacy A: Performance appraisal is the only process organizations use to describe, measure, and evaluate individuals' contributions.

Fallacy B: The primary goal of performance appraisal is to measure and rate performance.

Fallacy C: A well-designed performance appraisal system will always work as planned.

Fallacy D: Performance appraisal and performance feedback are one and the same.

Scenario A – Man Against The Machine

Performance Confrontations (Traditional Appraisals)

Manager: *Carlos, you met three of your four goals for the year and you exceeded expectations in almost every category on the appraisal.*
Employee: *I hope that you're not going to hold that against me.*
Manager: *What do you mean?*

Employee: *I didn't meet my sales totals because the Biodegrader II was having problems so it was harder to sell than last year.*

Manager: *I agree, but most of the other salespeople still managed to meet their totals.*

Employee: *Well, my customers bought a lot of them last year; that's why I was salesman of the year. Do you remember?*

Manager: *Yes, I remember.*

Employee: *So, there were two things working against me. I sold a lot last year so there were fewer companies in my territory to sell them to, and I didn't feel as confident in selling them this year with all of the problems that the system was having.*

Manager: *But, the technical problems with the system shouldn't have deterred you from selling it. The technical problems are being corrected by the Engineering department.*

Employee: *I know, but I didn't want to push the product as much, all things considered.*

Manager: *Either way, you did well overall.*

Employee: *So, you are going to hold it against me that I didn't meet the Biodegrader II sales goal?*

Performance Conversations®

Manager: *Carlos, you are doing well in three of the four goals we discussed at our Performance Planning session earlier this year.*

Employee: *I hope that you're not going to hold that against me.*

Manager: *What do you mean?*

Employee: *Things are going well. I'm pleased for the most part. However, I know that I haven't had as much luck selling the Biodegrader II lately.*

Manager: *Why?*

Employee: *The technical problems are a concern for many of my customers.*

Manager: *I understand that, however Engineering is correcting it and a patch should be available soon. Besides, the problems are only in one isolated area, and that small problem shouldn't effect the actual functioning of the machine.*

Employee: *Okay, but what should I say to my customers?*

Manager: *That the main part of the system is sound, and if they have any problems with it, we will either fix their system, replace their system, or give them a free year of technical support.*

Employee: *Great. That will make it easier to sell. But I still may not be able to sell as much as I have in the past.*

Manager: *Why?*

Employee: *Because last year I sold it to almost all of my customers, so there are fewer to sell to this year.*

Manager: *Should we expand your sales territory to give you some new leads?*
Employee: *Another great idea. This will give me the chance to become salesman of the year again. I enjoy selling products that I can believe in.*

Traditional appraisals pretend that the employee can affect their entire work environment and hold them accountable for things outside of their control. The Performance Conversations® approach recognizes that individual performance is partly due to the support they receive from the supervisor, the products they sell, their coworkers, and their environment, among other factors. By approaching performance management as a system, obstacles to the individual doing their very best work can be identified, dissected, and removed instead of assuming the individual is always at fault.

Fallacy A

The first thing to remember is that employee performance does not occur in a vacuum. We have to take a systems perspective and look not only at our employees, but also at the environments in which we expect them to perform. It has been said that if we put good performers in bad systems, the systems will win every time.
—David Ripley, "Improving Employee Performance," p.1

Fallacy A: Performance appraisal is the only process organizations use to describe, measure, and evaluate individuals' contributions.

Truth: The performance appraisal process is only one part of a larger organizational system that regulates performance.

Performance appraisals exist within the framework of an organization. The performance appraisal process is but a single element of the organization that regulates and manages overall performance. Other elements are the employees, culture, materials, equipment, methods, and structures (Coens and Jenkins, 2002).

The interdependent and multidimensional nature of an organization and its components are consistent with the ideas in *Systems Theory* (Senge, 1990). A systems theory view is that any system, be it the human body, an automobile, an organization, our economic system, or our eco-system, has interrelated parts that profoundly affect one another. Just as buying new tires will highlight shortcomings in the braking mechanism of a car, in any true system, the components are unequivocally connected in a variety of predictable and unpredictable ways.

Human Resource Management Practices Regulate Performance

Human Resources (HR) policies, programs, and practices all serve a strategic role in helping organizations compete effectively through the optimal employment of their people.

> Perhaps none of the resources used for productivity in organizations are so closely scrutinized as the human resources. Many of the activities undertaken in an HR system are designed to affect individual and organizational productivity. Pay, appraisal systems, training, selection, job design, and compensation are HR activities directly concerned with productivity.
> —Mathis and Jackson, *Human Resource Management*, p. 32

As an example, an organization that recruits only seasoned professionals must pay a higher-than-market wage to attract these veterans, but will likely need a lower-than-average training budget for seasoned talent. The performance outcomes of this organization will likely be better than for an organization that predominantly hires new college graduates. When the various HR programs within an organization are aligned with the mission, values, and goals of the organization, they support and enhance individual performance.

Organizational and Work Process Design Affect Individual Performance

The physical and structural design of the work in an organization defines the range of possible performance and productivity. An assembly line does not afford the same judgment, creativity, and expression of unlimited human potential as an employee in a quality circle. If an employee's input and range of contributions are limited through workflow design, the outputs possible are also limited. According to W. Edwards Deming, the work process also defines the type of problems employees will encounter and therefore can forecast the performance anomalies that can be expected.

> The performance of anybody is the result of a combination of many forces—the person himself, the people that he works with, the job, the material that he works on, his equipment, his customers, his management, his supervision, environmental conditions (noise, confusion, poor food in the company cafeteria).
> —Deming, *Out of Crisis*, p. 109

Managers must recognize that seldom is the employee the sole source of a performance challenge or seldom does the employee deserve complete credit for good performance. Each variable is an integrated part of a unified whole.

System Design Errors Can Produce Human Errors

A classic stereotype of a performance problem is when an hourly employee is told, "We do not pay you to think; just do it the way you were instructed." This response is frustrating and demoralizing. It is an unfortunate Catch-22 when a well-intentioned employee is disciplined for taking initiative to complete a task that is necessary to circumvent a poor system.

Other People Limit or Enhance an Individual Employee's Performance

All people connected to an organization affect the performance of each individual employee. In addition to supervisors, peers, subordinates, coworkers, and even customers help to regulate performance. Employees support, train, and give tips and advice to one another. The human dynamic within an organization can also work against performance when coworkers cause one another to fail. Hoarding information, avoiding those we personally dislike, not cooperating with one another, being competitive with one another, or otherwise not working as an interdependent team, are prime examples of failure points. Performance management systems should create an environment that recognizes and supports individuals working together. After all, working together is the idea of an "organization."

A manager who does not have good supervisory skills can obviously limit the potential of a good employee. However, an exceptional manager can bring out the best in someone.

Good Managers Create Good Performers

Any individual's performance is, to a considerable extent, a function of how he (or she) is managed.

—Kohn, *Punished By Rewards*, p. 129

Professional sports are filled with examples of an average player who changes teams and becomes a superstar under the direction of a different coach. A manager who does not have good supervisory skills can obviously limit the potential of a good employee. However, an exceptional manager can bring out the best in someone. To this point, Nicholson adds, "You (the manager) may be the main, if inadvertent, cause of your employee's lack of motivation; for one reason or another, you are bringing out the worst rather than the best in the person you are trying to help" (Nicholson, 2003, p. 29). The individual is the chief architect and major stakeholder in his own performance, but it would be shortsighted to think that the employee is alone in creating or affecting his performance. It is important for organizations to realize that when an employee is failing, the employee's performance, as well as that of the manager, needs to be considered as a part of the improvement plan.

Performance Problems Are Management Problems

W. Edwards Deming is said to have remarked about poor performers that "You either hired them that way or you made them that way." Regardless of the circumstance, managers are culpable for their employee's lackluster performance. If a manager has a poor performing employee, it should reflect upon the manager. Did the manager make a bad hire? Did the manager not orient and train the employee well? Did the manager not use proper supervision? Just as there is no simple correlation between what the manager did or did not do, there is no simple correlation between inadequate performance and the employee's efforts.

Are the tasks expected too difficult, unchallenging, or designed improperly? This is not to say that the employee is not responsible for his performance; however, if we start with the employee in all situations as the "problem," we might perpetuate a no-win situation. Because an individual employee is only one part of a larger system, she or he is only one variable in a potential problem and likewise, one part of a potential solution.

Organizational Culture Profoundly Affects Performance

Culture is the most important factor that regulates individual performance. The culture, values, and belief system of a company may drive or limit performance based on how the organization conducts daily business. The culture of an organization helps to describe for employees acceptable and unacceptable behaviors and performances. Culture defines the normative behavior of the entire organization.

Culture is the most important factor that regulates individual performance.

In addition to the type of performance that is defined by culture, culture also dictates the amount of effort and performance that is expected. A family-owned business may emphasize hard work and long hours because of the founder's Puritan work ethic. A financial services company may not have any scheduled work hours as long as brokers are exceeding performance targets. A manufacturing plant might have an outdated culture that practices the "honest day's work for an honest day's pay" philosophy. To the extent that culture regulates performance, a level of performance that garners recognition in one company may fall below the standard for another. Culture defines the standards and expectations of performance across all positions throughout the organization.

The Interdependent Nature of Performance Management

Like a leading actor in a play, the actor's performance is only as good as his leading lady, his fellow cast members, the stagehands, and musicians; his *coworkers*. His performance is also driven by the script and the score (environment), the stage production (work design), the lighting system (equipment), and the audience (customers), which gives the performer feedback as the play is being performed. The lead actor is only as good as the system in which he operates.

Solution: Design, adjust, and manage the organization as an interdependent system that supports performance. Integrate HR systems to include performance management, and align all performance management initiatives with the organizational culture and environment.

The solution to the fallacy that a performance appraisal instrument will cure all performance woes within an organization is to view the performance management process as a system with many components.

> In a system, all of the parts are interdependent. That is, a change in any part of a system will affect one or more other parts of that system. Hence, a system is not the sum of its parts; rather it is the sum of its parts plus the interaction of all of its parts. Because of the interdependency of the parts, improvement strategies aimed at the parts such as appraisal, do little or nothing to improve the system.
>
> —Coens and Jenkins, *Abolishing Performance Appraisals*, pp. 46–47

An analysis of the organization's culture is an important first step in managing performance. Is the performance in your organization, "good enough for government work," or is "quality job one"? What are the values, beliefs, and customs related to performance and behavior in your organization? Additionally, organizations should appreciate the degree to which supervision affects individual performance and should ensure that supervisors are capable of providing the needed support.

Performance Conversations® Building Blocks

The Performance Conversations® model incorporates the solution to Fallacy A by integrating performance management with good supervision. It recognizes that performance is multifaceted, and that a comprehensive approach to regulating performance is required to do it successfully. It also includes the most important quality assurance mechanism for performance—employee involvement. Multi-rater or 360 degree feedback is contained within Performance Conversations® when managers and employees note positive and negative customer, peer, and subordinate feedback in their **Performance Logs**. They include such proof in the **Performance Portfolio** through documents like thank you notes or written complaints. Instead of a supposed magical form that is the basis of traditional appraisal systems, the Performance Conversations® model is a comprehensive feedback system and management process.

Scenario B – Criminal Record?

Performance Confrontations (Traditional Appraisals)

Manager: *Mary, you had a good year except for the problems on the Amsterdam account.*

Employee: *I thought that was no longer a problem. I'm not sure why we have to bring that up. Didn't I fix that mistake?*

Manager: *Yes, you did fix it. You are doing A+ work now on all of your accounts. However, that problem happened during this reporting period. So, it is included in your total evaluation.*

Employee: *So, is it like I have a criminal record?*

Manager: *No!*

Employee: *Yes, it is. Somehow, it doesn't seem fair. I listened to you and learned from my mistake. The people in Amsterdam are happy and they are starting to become some of our top revenue producers. But are you saying that I won't get a good appraisal because of what happened last February? That was almost a year ago.*

Performance Conversations®

Manager: *Mary, I could not be more pleased. As I've looked back over the Performance Logs from the past year, it appears that we had a number of concerns early, but things improved.*

Employee: *Yes, I'm particularly proud of the fact that I learned a lot last year. The lessons I learned from the Amsterdam incident have made me a better account manager.*

Manager: *It was an impressive turn around.*

Employee: *Thanks, it was a joint effort.*

Manager: *Really?*

Employee: *Yes, your support and guidance was important in helping me refocus. The **Progress Reviews** were a great time for us to formally check in on the account and make continuous adjustments.*
Manager: *Well my role is to help you do your best.*
Employee: *Well, you made it easy by working with me each step of the way.*
Manager: *But you did the hard part.*
Employee: *Thank you; I did give it every effort.*

Traditional appraisals unnecessarily focus attention on the past. Performance Conversations® direct attention toward the future—the only performance that can be affected. These Conversations also happen at more frequent intervals so that issues can be addressed in a timely manner. Additionally, since a final rating is not required, work is viewed in a larger ongoing context. The focus is on continuous improvement, not past failures or successes.

Fallacy B

Fallacy B: The primary goal of performance appraisal is to measure and rate performance.

Truth: The real goals are to sustain good performance, improve performance, or correct poor performance.

Appraisals Look Backwards, Performance Is Prospective

Most of us do not have any control over the past; therefore, it is wiser to direct our attention and efforts towards improving the future. Our goals should be to continue good performance, correct performance, or improve it. Therefore, the implicit goal of performance appraisals is future oriented, not past oriented. Most appraisal systems mistakenly focus their attention on the past by emphasizing the rating of past performance.

Most appraisal systems mistakenly focus their attention on the past by emphasizing the rating of past performance.

Rating, Measurement, and Description

The rating process is actually a byproduct of the goal of measuring performance objectives. Except in a true production environment, measuring performance is a misguided effort. The real outcome that is sought in measuring performance is description. We want to describe or paint a picture of that which is good, better, best. When we accurately describe that which is preferred or expected, our thought is that we can replicate it. Examples of poor performance are highlighted, studied, analyzed, and hopefully avoided.

An accurate description or diagnosis leads to better prescriptions for future success. Why then do some measure performance as a means to an end? An important mantra for change in all organizations' performance management systems is: *the goal is feedback, not appraisal.* In current performance management systems, the supervisor's assessment (attempt at description) is fed back to the employee in hopes that the employee will acknowledge, understand, and act upon this information and then correct, sustain, or improve upon the performance. Unfortunately, this objective is rarely achieved.

The goal is feedback, not appraisal.

Grading Past Performance Does Not Change Past Performance

> Too often feedback gets mired in past transgressions. That makes the recipient feel bad—and defensive. The past is over. You want performance to improve the future. Give sufficient data about past performance so that the person understands your concern, then discuss how things could be different in the future.
>
> —Maurer, *The Feedback Toolkit*, p. 16

If a grade reflects anything below the best possible rating, individuals are left with questions regarding why they were not rated well and thoughts of how they could have done better. The outcome is consistent, employees are left to dwell on things they cannot change—the past. More profoundly, some argue that grading performance will motivate employees to do better in the future. Unlikely! We must also consider this sobering fact: that if grading performance can motivate, it can also de-motivate.

Even if grading past behavior could motivate future performance, would it not have been more effective to give this feedback at the time of the sub-standard performance events? Then the individual could have had months to change and improve performance. From my experience, many employees will simply ask, "Why tell me that I have provided B-plus performance now, when I wanted to give you A-plus service all along?"

Some argue that grading performance will motivate employees to do better in the future. Unlikely! We must also consider this sobering fact: that if grading performance can motivate, it can also de-motivate.

Verbal Feedback Is Better than Written Grades

If we must give employees grades—though I would argue that we never should—we should give grades verbally and at the time of the performance event. If an employee is *told* many times over the year that she is performing at a B-plus level, she has the opportunity to improve. She has time to ask "What else, or how else, must I work to get to A-plus service?" and take action. The timeliness of feedback gives the employee many opportunities for trial and error. The dialogue created facilitates defining ideal performance. Verbal grades are closer to feedback than evaluation. Verbal grades are likely to have less negative fallout than written grades that become a part of the dreaded "permanent personnel record."

Self-Assessments are Effective Exercises, not Effective Instruments

Many performance appraisal systems require employees to prepare a self-assessment and reflect upon their efforts over the reporting period. If the goal is for the employee to be engaged in the recognition, description, analysis, and interpretation of their efforts, self-assessments are somewhat magical in their ability to affect performance. If the goal is that the self-assessment becomes a part of the permanent record, then it is a bad idea. Asking one to rate their performance at anything less than a good rating that will help them get a raise or a reward is more closely akin to an IQ test than a performance evaluation.

Incentives are based upon the basic psychological principle that individuals will act in their own best interest. If we assume the false notion that people are selfish and self-serving, the idea of self-evaluations is unsound. If pay is tied to performance and an employee is tasked with evaluating himself, why would one assign a rating that would lower the chances of getting a merit increase?

Pick one, because both cannot be true:

- If we believe employees will only act in their own self-interest, it is not likely that they will provide a pool of information to be used against them.

- If we do not expect people to act in their own selfish interest, then this refutes the theory upon which incentives are predicated.

Either way, if an employee is threatened by the use of the information, or feels that her honesty will be used against her, it is only human to withhold unflattering information from the manager, regardless of whether the information is useful or not for improving their performance.

Solution: The performance management process should be future oriented and focused on information, feedback, and description rather than measurement, evaluation, and documentation.

Performance management systems should eliminate the emphasis on measurement and rating, and instead focus on performance improvement almost exclusively. Systems should be future oriented. Efforts should be placed on generating open dialogue to uncover the core elements of performance. The focus of documenting the past should be replaced with working together on diagnosing problems, replicating successes, and creating future successes.

Performance Conversations® Building Blocks

The Performance Conversations® model incorporates the solution to Fallacy B by using frequent *Progress Reviews* to determine what performance to correct, what performance to keep, and how to generally improve performance. Feedback and information about past performance information are shared and analyzed during these conversations. This information is used to focus attention and efforts on future performance instead of trying to document what happened in the past like traditional appraisals.

Scenario C – I Wrote It Myself

Performance Confrontations (Traditional Appraisals)

Manager: *Paul, could you redo the third and four paragraphs of your evaluation?*
Employee: *No problem, did I come on a little too strong?*
Manager: *No, it just sounds a little too good.*
Employee: *I wasn't sure what you wanted, so I wrote it from my memory.*
Manager: *Paul, I really appreciate you taking the first step to draft a summary of your past year's annual review. You know that I've been taxed by the upcoming building project. While it might be accurate, it is so good that it doesn't look like you have any areas to improve upon. That will not fly with HR. We need to identify*

some areas for improvement. So, that's why I suggested that you cut out some of the things in those two paragraphs.

Employee: *But, those are some of my best areas of work.*

Manager: *These reviews don't really matter. We just need something for the files.*

Employee: *But it wouldn't be totally accurate. I must admit I was a bit uncomfortable when you initially asked me to draft part of my own annual review. Now, I'm even more uncomfortable changing the things I wrote about myself because I think they accurately reflect my work. I mean, you shouldn't ask me to write it and then tell me it isn't about being accurate, but about it passing the audit from Human Resources.*

Manager: *Paul, everybody knows that you are our best performer. This form won't change anything.*

Employee: *Okay, then let's just not do it…and tell HR that all is well so we can get back to real work.*

Performance Conversations®

Manager: *How are things going?*

Employee: *Good.*

Manager: *Tell me this, how do we know that things are going well?*

Employee: *Because, I haven't made any mistakes.*

Manager: *Well, we should be able to prove to ourselves what is going well, so that we know what to keep doing. And we both should be able to recognize things that aren't going well so that we can fix them. How can we prove things are going well?*

Employee: *My quarterly report shows all the totals for the year in comparison to past years.*

Manager: *Good! What else?*

Employee: *I've received two thank you notes from customers, and Betty from Accounting called to thank me for my help last week.*

Manager: *Those are good examples. Do you have any copies of these? Are they written down anywhere?*

Employee: *No. I just know they happened.*

Manager: *How about if you keep notes, copies, or any other documents* [**Performance Portfolio**] *like these. We can meet periodically* [**Progress Reviews**] *to talk about all of the information that you gather and I gather as well?*

Employee: *That would be a good way for me to prove that things are going well.*

Manager: *That's the idea.*

Supervisors who do not take performance management seriously undermine their own ability to supervise subordinates and to regulate their productivity. The Performance Conversations® approach makes performance management a shared responsibility. The employee expects to track (Performance Logs, Performance Portfolios) and monitor (Progress Reviews) their own performance and to give and receive feedback with the supervisor. This creates a system of checks and balances.

Fallacy C

Fallacy C: A well-designed performance appraisal system will always work as planned.

Truth: A process that is not used (or used improperly) by managers and employees is useless.

The Best That Money Can Buy

Even the most sophisticated appraisal system designed by the most expensive consultants will not work if the managers do not complete the instruments conscientiously and on time. Incomplete, late, forgotten, avoided, or trivialized evaluations are an insult to the employee. When all subordinates are given the same evaluation or when favoritism exists, it completely undermines the credibility of traditional evaluation systems. Each of these shortcomings in the completion of appraisals causes them to be neither useful nor effective.

Inconsistent Use of Appraisals Reduces the Credibility of the System

If performance appraisals are not completed in the marketing department, employees in the operations department will doubt the importance of the process to management. If Jane, the department's superstar, is allowed to perform well but treat fellow teammates poorly, then her peers will not believe the supervisor's rating of their attitude or the ability to get along with coworkers. Inconsistent use of appraisals will offend employees' sense of fairness and justice. If rewards such as pay or recognition are then tied to inconsistently applied evaluations, managers will lose the trust and confidence of their employees. The overall process will not have credibility or value and will, without question, lower morale.

Results Not Utilized Sends the Message That the Process is not Worthwhile

Many completed evaluations are filed away and never used. Supervisors who know that the results are meaningless are often overheard telling employees that the appraisal is completed only because "We are *required* to complete the form."

If the results are not used in a meaningful manner, the tool is neither credible nor useful, and managers and employees know this to be true.

Even if an appraisal review session is conducted, it is not effective if it is not the culminating point of a series of conversations with the employee over the entire review period.

Close but No Cigar—Once-a-Year Appraisal is Not a Substitute for Regular Feedback

Even if an appraisal review session is conducted, it is not effective if it is not the culminating point of a series of conversations with the employee over the entire review period. Feedback or appraisal that occurs once or twice a year is not enough. To be effective, a performance management system must have both informal and formal elements and must be conducted in an ongoing and periodic fashion. A single annual feedback session is virtually ineffective.

Avoiding Appraisals

Another reason performance appraisals are not completed is that managers and employees often avoid them. Appraisals are avoided particularly when managers must communicate negative information. "Because supervisors often feel uncomfortable taking even clearly appropriate disciplinary action, they often hesitate until there is no alternative" (Grote, 1995, p. 17). Research shows that managers dread doing performance evaluations as much as employees dislike participating in them. When managers procrastinate or attempt to avoid appraisals, it ultimately leads to late appraisals.

Late Evaluations

Human resources or personnel chase the forms, hoping to achieve an eighty-percent-plus return rate, and are satisfied when this happens. Often, forms are collected well after the deadline to accommodate postponed interviews.
—Lecky-Thompson, *Constructive Appraisals*, p. 24

Many managers complete all of their appraisals the day before they are due to be submitted to the HR department. Sometimes, the evaluations were due months before, but in order for an employee to get a raise, the form must be sent in to the HR department. When performance appraisals are prepared like cramming for a test, they are usually incomplete and inaccurate, yielding a process that is increasingly trivialized.

A Trivialized Formal Process

Neal offers a candid assessment of some managers' behavior as he reports, "Weak managers downplay the importance of appraisals by making them appear to be trivial" (Neal, 2001, p. 131). Here are several recognizable quips from managers who devalue the importance of a performance appraisal process. They are quite recognizable!

- "You did a good, job keep it up; here, sign this."

- "You know how I feel about your work; this form does not matter."

- "I put your evaluation in your box; let's schedule an appointment if you want to talk about any of it."

- "We talk every day. An appraisal form is not going to tell us anything new."

- "With the rating I gave you, you will get an above average raise this year."

- "We are too busy making money to complete those %#$# @! evaluation forms."

"Everyone Is Excellent In My Department" or "No One Is Perfect"

> Easier graders undermine appraisal systems—and morale.
> —Mariotti, "Tough Bosses, Easy Bosses," p. 1

One of the significant problems with performance appraisal systems is that there is no universal definition of what is *good* or *bad*. This difficulty is exacerbated when the work is different across the various departments of an organization. Herein lies one of the major, if not the most significant, shortcomings in the use of performance appraisals. Very lenient managers give all of their subordinates an outstanding rating because all the employees are *good* people. However, identical ratings can also be given when the manager does not have the fortitude to confront poorly performing employees in a proper manner. A tough manager, who believes that *no one is perfect,* never gives any employee, regardless of performance, a perfect score. The personal philosophy of this manager overrides the training and expectations for the use of the performance management system. The subordinates in this department may suffer the loss of promotional and income opportunities because the manager has set a performance standard that can never be met.

Solution: Hold supervisors accountable for their staff development, supervision, results, and participation in the performance management process (completed, on time, and accurate).

The performance management process must be taken seriously and timely participation must be required of all managers and employees. Otherwise, the performance management system will not be viewed with any credibility within the organization. This is truly the occasion when one weak link will undermine the efficacy of the entire system. Managers must be held accountable for their full participation in the performance management process.

Performance Conversations® Building Blocks

The Performance Conversations® model addresses Fallacy C by making the employee co-owner of the performance management process. The manager and the employee co-perform; meaning their responsibilities and outcomes are joint responsibilities. The employee is expected to give and receive feedback to and from the supervisor, so if the supervisor does not do his or her part the employee makes notes of this in their **Performance Log**. The employee documents the obstacles to her success and shares these concerns with the manager in **Progress Reviews**. Employee involvement helps to hold the supervisor accountable for timely, complete, and accurate performance feedback, as opposed to traditional appraisals where the supervisor's failure to give periodic feedback and complete an annual form is seldom addressed by senior management.

Scenario D – I Thought I Was Doing Okay

Performance Confrontations (Traditional Appraisals)

Manager: *Things haven't been as good as they could have been these last few months.*
Employee: *What?*
Manager: *There are some areas of improvement that I would like for you to work on.*
Employee: *I thought I was doing okay.*
Manager: *You are doing pretty good, but I' have some concerns.*
Employee: *I haven't heard anything negative from you since my last performance appraisal six months ago.*
Manager: *I didn't want to discourage or demotivate you.*
Employee: *I wish you had said something earlier. I would have tried harder.*
Manager: *Maybe you should try—*

Employee: *It is a little late for that now. I wish I had known all along that you weren't satisfied with my work. I thought that "no news was good news."'*

Performance Conversations®

Manager: *Things haven't been as good as they could have been these last few months.*

Employee: *I agree.*

Manager: *We have talked several times, to include at our last **Progress Review** about your work on the new software. We continue to be behind. You do know that I have some concerns.*

Employee: *I know. But we keep running into technical glitches.*

Manager: *What kind of technical glitches?*

Employee: *Every time we get ready to implement a new module, we get error messages on our practice runs.*

Manager: *Is there anything I can do to assist you?*

Employee: *I'm not sure what that would be or how you can help.*

Manager: *Because we are falling behind, I'm going to ask that I get a weekly report from you every Friday. If things are not going well, I would like to know as problems occur. If you need help, more resources, or anything please let me know as soon as possible.*

Employee: *Thank you for the offer. But only I can run the tests. I might have to put in a few nights or weekends to get the project back on schedule.*

Manager: *You aren't in this alone. I will do all that I can do to assist you, but we must communicate more to ensure that we are meeting our deadlines.*

Traditional appraisals offer one or two review sessions annually in which the manager shares information with the employee about their performance. These infrequent occasions are not enough to "manage" performance. In the Performance Conversations® approach, there are several planned, structured opportunities (**Progress Reviews**) to discuss performance parameters and to make necessary adjustments. These occasions are not designed to label performance but instead to generate enough information (feedback) to help create and replicate good performance.

Fallacy D

Performance review is the worst time to give feedback to an employee. You are nervous and the recipient is taking an acid bath. These conditions are not conducive to a productive conversation about performance.

—Maurer, *The Feedback Toolkit*, p. 12

Fallacy D: Performance appraisal and performance feedback are one and the same.

Truth: Appraisal is judgment; feedback is useful information.

While many may confuse the two, feedback and appraisal are fundamentally different activities. Feedback is information based, while the basis of an appraisal is judgment or evaluation.

While many may confuse the two, feedback and appraisal are fundamentally different activities. Feedback is information based, while the basis of an appraisal is judgment or evaluation. Feedback is expected to be an ongoing activity, and appraisal is assumed to be periodic and event based. Feedback should occur as often as possible, and appraisal is expected to happen once or twice a year. There are other differences in the two activities, but the point made here is that feedback and appraisal are not a single activity; this point is imperative in performance management, it is not merely a matter of semantics.

Chart 2.1 summarizes some well-documented perceptual differences in the activities.

| TYPICAL CHARACTERISTICS OF . . . ||
Feedback	Appraisal
Information	Judgment, Evaluation
Ongoing, Continuous	Periodic, Event-based
Daily	Semi-annually, Annually
Immediate	Retrospective
Informal	Formal
Verbal	Written
Builds trust and relationships	Inhibits trust, harms relationships
Not linked to rewards and punishments	Linked to rewards and punishments
Potentially positive connotation	Potentially negative connotations
Generally neutral or positive reaction	Potential emotional reaction

Chart 2.1

Appraisal is not a neutral activity, it highlights differences in power and authority and it is most often causes a variety of emotional reactions.

Feedback, Not Appraisal

"Feedback is the primary means for recognizing good performance and for redirecting behavior than needs to be improved. Feedback helps individuals to keep their behavior on target and achieve their goals" (Costello, 1994, p. 50). Appraisal cannot be substituted for feedback; they are neither synonymous nor interchangeable. A pearl of wisdom from The *One-Minute Manager* shines clear, "Feedback is the Breakfast of Champions" (Blanchard and Lober, 1984, p. 66). Employees want *feedback*, not *appraisal*.

Formal and Informal Feedback

Ongoing feedback as performance events occur should be complemented by periodic opportunities to step back and look at performance trends. Informal and frequent feedback is as essential as semi-annual or periodic formal feedback. Both are necessary, but not sufficient alone. There is no good alternative to frequent performance information shared between the employee and their manager.

There is no good alternative to frequent performance information shared between the employee and their manager.

Solution: Formal, informal, ongoing, periodic, micro-level and macro-level feedback should all be used to manage performance.

If appraisal is the only source of feedback, then it is virtually useless for managing and directing performance and behavior. There should be formal and informal mechanisms within an organization to share information about performance. Likewise, there should be immediate, frequent, and ongoing performance feedback shared on a day-to-day or short-term basis. In addition, there should be periodic feedback at a macro level over longer periods of time that summarizes, determines, and analyzes performance trends. In any event, the emphasis should be on the sharing of information instead of the evaluation thereof.

Performance Conversations® Building Blocks

One of the strongest elements of the Performance Conversations® model is its ability to give both general and specific feedback. *Performance Logs* keep employees and supervisors focused on the things that matter each day. This information is used to regulate performance as it occurs. The sharing of feedback at Progress Reviews is conversational and semi-formal, yet fluid enough to correct problems while they are small and structured enough to deal with larger issues as necessary. Annual Performance Analysis and Summary sessions provide a formal occasion to discuss trends and macro-level feedback. The Performance Conversations® model follows the advice contained in the solution to Fallacy D as opposed to traditional performance appraisals which attempt to manage and regulate performance through a single annual review.

Summary of the Fallacies of Purpose

Performance appraisals exist within a larger organizational context and are but one element within a larger system that regulates individual performance. The culture and values of an organization and the quality of supervision will affect performance and productivity. The human resources policies and procedures will stand with or stand in contrast to what performance is expected and is valued, so all organizational components must be aligned with its mission and goals.

Managers must be trained well for their role as supervisors and must be held accountable for their participation in the performance management process. Even the best performance management system is useless if managers do not use it, and use it correctly. Employees should not be given mixed signals about what is good or bad or what is expected and valued; all organizational systems should reinforce one another and support individual performance.

Performance appraisals should be replaced with a process for performance improvement that is focused on the future instead of the past. The emphasis on measurement and documentation should be replaced with a process of generating information used to create better conversations, work conditions, and successes. The emphasis should be on feedback not appraisal. Performance management systems should create opportunities for formal and informal information exchange and cooperation.

Fallacy A: Performance appraisal is the only process organizations use to describe, measure, and evaluate individuals' contributions.

Truth: The performance appraisal process is only one part of a larger system that regulates performance.

Solution: Design, adjust, and manage the organization as an interdependent system that supports performance. Integrate HR systems to include performance management, and align all performance management initiatives with the organizational culture and environment.

Fallacy B: The primary goal of performance appraisal is to measure and rate performance.

Truth: The real goals are to sustain good performance, improve performance, or correct poor performance.

Solution: The performance management process should be future oriented and focused on information, feedback, and description rather than measurement, evaluation, and documentation.

Fallacy C: A well-designed performance appraisal system will always work as planned.

Truth: A process that is not used (or used improperly) by managers and employees is useless.

Solution: Hold supervisors accountable for their staff development, supervision, results, and participation in the performance management process (completed, on time, and accurate).

Fallacy D: Performance appraisal and performance feedback are one and the same.

Truth: Appraisal is judgement; feedback is useful information.

Solution: Formal, informal, ongoing, periodic, micro-level and macro-level feedback should all be used to manage performance.

Quick Reference Points

Chapter 4

- The culture, coworkers, HR policies and procedures, equipment, work design, and other organizational elements all affect individual performance.

- Supervision can enhance or diminish individual performance.

- Appraisals document the past, but the past cannot be changed.

- The real goals of performance management are to improve future performance, correct bad performance, and sustain good performance.

- Self-assessments can be effective if they are not used to grade performance.

- Performance description and problem diagnosis are better than rating and measurement.

- Appraisals do not work because managers avoid them, don't do them, or do them poorly.

- Frequent informal feedback is better than once-a-year appraisal.

- Feedback, not appraisal, is an important concept (Reread that section).

- Feedback manages performance, appraisal evaluates and documents the past.

False Assumptions

THE THOUGHT PROCESS AND the science behind the use of performance appraisal are questionable. This chapter identifies four false assumptions about performance and performance appraisal. Once we acknowledge these falsities, we will better understand why the various uses, designs, and goals associated with performance appraisal are fundamentally flawed.

Managers in the past fifty years have not applied as sound psychological principles to performance appraisals as they have to other human and organizational endeavors. McGregor offered this statement dozens of years ago:

> I have sought to show that the conventional approach to performance appraisal stands condemned as a personnel method. It places the manager in the untenable position of judging the personal worth of his subordinates, and of acting on these judgments. No manager possesses, nor could he acquire, the skill necessary to carry out this responsibility effectively. Few would even be willing to accept it if they were fully aware of the implications involved.
> —McGregor, "An Uneasy Look at Performance Appraisal," p. 6

Only with new thinking and better assumptions can we design better systems. The first and most startling false assumption is that organizations can motivate people to perform. Fifty years of research have proven that the carrot and stick method does not work to generate and sustain quality performance. Alfie Kohn (1993) and others have spent a great deal of time communicating just this point. Here we will offer only a few counterpoints, since an in-depth exploration of this topic is beyond the scope of this book. However, if you want more information on the subject just go to my website www.performanceconversations.com. Those who would argue this point further will ignore many advances in social science.

These are the fallacies collectively considered to be false assumptions:

Fallacy E: Appropriately designed incentives will motivate employees to perform.

Fallacy F: Rating (or grading) performance is sound management practice.

Fallacy G: Performance appraisals are a necessary evil.

Fallacy H: Appraisals are necessary for documentation and administrative decisions.

The solutions to each of the fallacies throughout this chapter will be used to create and justify the Performance Conversations® model.

Scenario E – I Don't Work For Money

Performance Confrontations (Traditional Appraisals)

Manager: *Brenda, you always do a good job. Everyone knows you have a long history of success with Birmingham Metal Works.*

Employee: *Thank you, Mr. Hawkins. I always try to do my very best.*

Manager: *There is one issue I do want to discuss with you, though!*

Employee: *What's that?*

Manager: *You consistently did well last year, just like the year before and the year before as that. However, I'm disappointed that your numbers didn't go up at all.*

Employee: *Was there a problem that I don't know about?*

Manager: *No, there wasn't any problem. I was just disappointed that your output did not go up during our promotion while almost everyone else's did.*

Employee: *Well, I don't pay attention to any of those "management" promotions.*

Manager: *Really? Why not?*

Employee: *First, I don't need the money; I work to get out of the house and have enough money to buy nice things for my grandkids. Second, I do a good job all the time whether there is a promotion going on or not. Is there a problem with my performance?*

Manager: *No, there isn't any real problem. But we had hoped that with the promotion all of our individual numbers would go up, and so would the department's.*

Employee: *Mr. Hawkins, you can count on me to work hard for you all of the time. When there is a promotion going on, I'm going to work hard. When there aren't any bonuses tied to what I do, then I'm going to work hard then as well. I'm too old to jump through hoops. If you are saying that I'm not doing well enough, I might need to retire. But if I'm doing okay, I'm not sure what the fuss is all about.*

Performance Conversations®

Manager: *Brenda, you always do a good job. Everyone knows you have a long history of success with Birmingham Metal Works.*

Employee: *Thank you, Mr. Hawkins. I always try to do my very best.*

Manager: *You are consistent and we can always count on you to be above average in every category of orders processed. But what can I do to support you more or better?*

Employee: *Nothing really. I enjoy my work. I like the people, and you have always helped me when I had questions. So, I'm okay, I'm just happy doing a good job.*

Manager: *That's positive, but are there any challenges, goals, or opportunities that would interest you?*

Employee: *There is one thing now that you mention it. I would like to take a few computer courses. I know just enough to do my work, but if I were to learn more stuff, it might help me process orders faster. I'm not sure if it would help, but it couldn't hurt.*

Manager: *I will set some training up for you.*

Employee: *But, I would really like one-on-one training. I get intimidated going to those big classrooms with a lot of youngsters who already know more than I will ever learn.*

Manager: *Brenda, we value you as a person and as a staff member. We will get you any and all of the training that you want. It would be my pleasure to arrange it.*

The Performance Conversations model relies on an individual's natural desire to do well and their pride in their workmanship. This Theory Y approach nurtures their internal drive without using the false promise of incentives to manipulate their performance. Motivation comes from within; the manager's primary responsibility is to create the environment and conditions that allows the individual's natural ability to manifest itself.

Fallacy E

Fallacy E: Appropriately designed incentives will motivate employees to perform better.

Truth: Motivation is intrinsic; extrinsic motivation has very limited effectiveness.

For mindless jobs, extrinsic rewards beyond pay and benefits often serve as surrogates for job design; i.e. instead of redesigning a job to make it more intrinsically rewarding, we distract workers by offering them 'prizes' for hanging in there and behaving themselves. It's a kindergarten approach to behavior modification in the workplace. And once the music stops, they stop dancing! Surprise! Surprise!

—Benham, Letter to the author, p. 3

People Are Not Machines

The premise behind using incentives is that employees will not do, or do not do, what they are instructed, so management must induce, motivate, manipulate, control, threaten, punish, reward, or persuade them to perform in a prescribed manner. This harmful perspective causes management to treat employees like children, animals, or machines. Many motivational systems are based on behaviorism or the belief that all employees subject to a random management intervention will react as expected and will be motivated in a manner that was planned and designed. Provide one unit of input into the person, and out comes the desired product or output. This theory assumes people will somehow react like animals or well-calibrated machines each and every time a carrot is offered.

Incentives and Rewards Motivate Only For a Minute or Two!

Incentives have limited use and limited effectiveness.

> Smart managers understand that the subject of incentives is complex. As noted above, some experts maintain that incentives are ineffective for improving long-term performance, particularly if incentives are removed after having been in place for some specified period. They argue that performance actually deteriorates over time; further, incentives not only direct attention away from the inherent satisfaction that comes from work itself toward the stars, prizes, and cash awards of immediate gratification, but also have an adverse impact on motivation. And the experts have data to support their claims.
>
> Others maintain that incentives are vital to increasing productivity and that without them employees will have little or no inclination to improve performance. Indeed, they contend, employees are fundamentally lazy and their motivation comes only from rewards.
>
> Regardless of their persuasion, on one key point experts on both sides of the issue agree: *incentives influence increased performance in the short term.*
> —Bowen, *Recognizing and Rewarding Employees*, pp. 32–33

Incentives may be effective in the short term, however, there are *significant* long-term costs associated with any short-term gains.

Rewards and Incentives Can Have a Negative Effect

If rewards are provided as a result of competition, inevitably somebody has to lose. The losers are left dejected or demoralized, or at the very least unhappy. Furthermore, rewards are often coupled with punishment. The signals are clear—act, perform, or behave in a manner sought by management and you get a carrot; if you do not, you get a stick. In either outcome, the presence of rewards in these scenarios is accompanied by fear. There is also the message that coworkers are *the enemy*. After all, "Only one of us can get the reward." This is not effective in building teamwork.

Rational Employees and Desirable Rewards

> The use of incentives also assumes that employees are rational and that their behavior follows a rational pattern in their best interest.

The use of incentives also assumes that employees are rational and that their behavior follows a rational pattern in their best interest. If only this were true! This series of assumptions is not true for employees or human beings in general. Examples of such human behavior as smoking, drinking, or eating to excess would illustrate that people do not always do what is in their best interest. Even if incentives worked, managers would have a difficult time finding the right incentive for the right person on the right occasion.

Does Money Motivate?

People need money to live, but we do not live for money. Most of us are driven to make a difference and to contribute to something greater than ourselves. Frederick Herzberg noted decades ago that money was a hygiene factor and that while its absence was a de-motivator, its presence was not a motivator. Nonetheless, many organizations are still trying unsuccessfully to influence employee performance with financial incentives.

If money were a prime motivator, then people would join, perform for, and stay with an organization for slight differences in pay. In contrast, they may also not join, not perform, and leave an organization for the same slight financial difference. If this were true, people would only seek jobs and professions that paid the most money. They would not work in professions that are valued less by labor markets. People would neither seek work that interested them, nor would they be motivated to do a job in which they could excel. Their focus would be on the most lucrative work. Nonprofit organizations would suffer since they generally pay less than for-profit companies, even for identical jobs.

> If money and incentives are not the root of all organizational performance evils, they are at least the basis for a lot of misplaced time and effort.

In addition to the many studies that have proven that money is not a prime motivator, there are studies that indicate attempting to use money to motivate employees may produce the opposite or even negative effects.

> Despite the evident popularity of this practice, the problems with individual merit pay are numerous and well documented. It has been shown to undermine teamwork, encourage employees to focus on the short term, and lead people to link compensation to poor skills and ingratiating personalities rather than performance.
>
> —Pfeffer-Stanford, "Six Dangerous Myths about Pay," p. 7

If money and incentives are not the root of all organizational performance evils, they are at least the basis for a lot of misplaced time and effort.

Motivation Is Intrinsic

The fallacies surrounding motivation are a hot topic for many business books.

> Everybody knows that good managers motivate with the power of their vision, the passion of their delivery, and the compelling logic of their reasoning. Add in the proper incentives, and people enthusiastically march off in the right direction.
>
> It's a great image, promoted in stacks of idealistic leadership books. But something is seriously wrong with it. Such a strategy works with only a fraction of employees and a smaller fraction of managers. . . . [A]ll available evidence suggests that external incentives—be they pep talks, wads of cash, or even the threat of unpleasant consequences—have limited impact. The people who might respond to such inducements are already up and running. It's the other folks who are the problem.
>
> —Nicholson, *Harvard Business Review on Motivating People*, pp. 20–21

It is widely acknowledged in management circles that motivation is intrinsic and that performance appraisals are limited, if not completely ineffective, in their application. However, in a classic case of doublespeak, many authors avoid these almost universal truths and offer supposed ways of getting around these fundamental facts. The truth is that we cannot ignore the facts. We must embrace them and design performance management systems that take them into full consideration. Motivation is intrinsic—we must help employees realize their potential, not by trying to control them with persuasion or coercion, but rather through partnership, support, nurturing, and respect.

If we believe that we cannot manipulate people with incentives and threats, then our basic assumptions regarding how we work with others will be permanently altered.

Motivation is truly an "inside" job. No one can make you do something against your will. You may do something you don't particularly want to do, but if won't be against your will. You may be confronted with some extremely hard choices, but what you decide to do is ultimately your decision.

—Bowen, *Recognizing and Rewarding Employees*, p. 30

People naturally want to do well. Metaphorically speaking, intrinsic motivation is similar to a river flowing, and we should design organizations that work with the river's natural currents. If we continue to design systems that attempt to control, manipulate, or force employees to do things against their nature, we will always paddle upstream.

Motivation is intrinsic—we must help employees realize their potential, not by trying to control them with persuasion or coercion, but rather through partnership, support, nurturing, and respect.

Solution: Providing challenging, meaningful work, creating a nurturing and supportive environment, and involving employees in decisions that affect their work—these imperatives encourage pride in workmanship and personal growth. This is the key to sustained motivation.

Performance Conversations® Building Blocks

The spirit of Fallacy E is included in the Performance Conversations® model because employees are involved in every phase of their work, and therefore are empowered to create their ideal work environment. Employees are challenged by the responsibility and ownership of their efforts, behaviors, and outcomes. Furthermore, the environment created by collegial conversation, partners working together toward common goals, and freedom from the fear of punishment are indicative of a positive and nurturing relationship. The communication, collaboration and cooperation that fuels Performance Conversations® sets them apart from traditional appraisals that assume that employees will not do what they are supposed to do, so they are given incentives to work, watched, and treated like they are not trustworthy. The **prerequisites** to good performance management outlined in Chapter 9 also help to create the right climate for productive Performance Conversations® to occur.

Good Work Is a Reward in and of Itself, and the Real Motivator

Building upon Theory Y ideas that people are naturally inclined to be productive, to excel, and to make positive contributions to their families, their organizations, and to society, organizations of the future will create the right conditions to support these inherent characteristics of the human spirit. This will allow positive contributions to occur naturally and without prompting. Today, many high-performing organizations achieve better results than their competitors simply by the thoughtful design of work, valued treatment of employees, and by ensuring that their policies and procedures create a positive and supportive environment. They also incorporate such solid HR practices and principles into interactions with employees as providing challenging work, involving employees in decisions, and sharing responsibility for work efforts and outcomes. This gives employees all the motivation they need to do well and sustain good performance.

Here are a few quotes from various experts that I think describe very well the conditions that create natural employee motivation:

> Most of all, a manager committed to making sure that people are able and willing to do their best needs to attend to three fundamental factors. These can be abbreviated as the "three Cs" of motivation — to wit, the *collaboration* that defines the context of the work, the *content* of the tasks, and the extent to which people have some *choice* about what they do and how they do it.
>
> —Kohn, *Punished by Rewards*, p. 187

> People do not want another form. They do want challenge, trust, a work climate that balances freedom and support, and genuine appreciation for their unique talents and contributions.
>
> —Coens and Jenkins, *Abolishing Performance Appraisals*, p. xx

> Motivators, on the other hand, are found primarily in the nature of the work itself. Jobs that are seen by their incumbents as challenging and offering variety, significance, and whole pieces of work with some measure of autonomy and feedback are most likely to motivate commitment to the job and efforts to improve job performance.
>
> —J. Hackman and G. Oldman, "Motivation through the Design of Work"

> When people are intrinsically motivated, they engage in their work for the challenge and enjoyment of it. The work itself is motivation.... people will be most creative when they are motivated primarily by interest, satisfaction, and challenge of the work itself—not by external pressures.
>
> —Amabile, *How to Kill Creativity*, p. 3

> Intrinsically motivating employment entails jobs that possess task significance, skill variety, task identity (a clear work product), performance feedback and worker autonomy.
>
> —Roberts, "Employee Performance Appraisal System Participation," p. 2

In addition to the quotes above, the following chart summarizes the ideas of scores of authors:

Characteristics that Create an Ideal Work Situation	
The Work Itself (good jobs)	The Work Environment (the Culture)
Rich job content	Trust
Interesting work	Support
Increasing responsibility	Environment that includes caring
Challenge	Genuine appreciation
Achievement	Collaboration on work-related issues
Use of various skills at work	Choice about what is done and how it is done
Variety of tasks within a particular job	Positive and enjoyable work climate
Holistic work (a clear work product)	Performance feedback
Satisfying work	Recognition for achievement
Important work	Opportunity for growth
Freedom and autonomy to act	Opportunity for advancement

Figure 3.1

These ideas are foundational principles for the Performance Conversations® model. Collectively they illustrate how people should be treated within organizations—essentially a twenty-first-century version of Theory Y management. The goal is to harness human potential in a nurturing and humane manner that is natural, self-regenerating, and mutually beneficial to the individual, organization, and society.

Scenario F – I Deserve An "A+"

Performance Confrontations (Traditional Appraisals)

Manager: *"Chin, I think that you performed exceptionally well last year. You led the pack and performed better than everyone in the department."*
Employee: *"I have also been happy with how things were going. It has been a good year."*
Manager: *"So I'm pleased to give you a "4.8 of 5," which, according to our scale indicates exceptional or meritorious service. You deserve it."*

Employee: *"Shouldn't I get a 5?"*

Manager: *"I gave you the highest score of everyone in the department."*

Employee: *"Thank you. But shouldn't my overall evaluation be a 5.0? You gave me 5's on all of the individual scales, so why is my overall score a 4.8?"*

Manager: *"Well, I'm giving you a 4.8 because we all have areas to improve upon."*

Employee: *"But if I'm the best, and I got all 5's on the first page, I don't understand how things could be different on the final score!"*

Performance Conversations®

Manager: *"Chin, I think that you performed exceptionally well last year. You led the pack and performed better than everyone in the department."*

Employee: *"I have also been happy with how things were going. It has been a good year."*

Manager: *"Why do you think you performed so well last year?"*

Employee: *"I'm not sure. I just started feeling more confident each day about my work."*

Manager: *"I think that the team leader training that you attended last year made a difference."*

Employee: *"Yes, I learned to focus more on helping others do their part. When I learned to delegate and empower my teammates, I then had more time to plan and monitor their efforts."*

Manager: *"So, how can we ensure that your success and your team's success continues into the coming year?"*

Employee: *"Hmmm . . . well, I could spend more time with the team members who are not doing as well as the rest of the team. According to the reports here in the* **Performance Portfolio**, *there is a clear pattern that one third barely meets their targets, one-third do well, and one-third do well most of the time, but slip every now and again."*

Manager: *"A good place to start would be to find out why the third group falls behind sometime. Knowing why might help the slower group as well."*

Employee: *"That would be a good start. I enjoy our periodic* **Performance Conversations®**, *they give us a chance to discuss real issues, diagnose problems, and find better ways of working."*

Manager: *"I enjoy them as well, especially since you are always open and willing to discuss important things with me before they become bigger issues."*

Ratings or labels direct attention away from the work toward the defense of what is meant by 'good' or 'great'. The Supervisor has to justify down to a minute degree what their definition of 'good' is. If the employee's perspective differs from the manager's, a problem occurs. Nonetheless, in the Performance Conversations® approach, attention is focused on one thing—future performance. Performance is discussed and analyzed, and the result is used to improve performance instead of quantifying the past.

Fallacy F

Fallacy F: Rating (or grading) performance is sound management.

Truth: Rating performance reflects Theory X management.

The poor track record and widespread dissatisfaction with appraisal as a rating device are well documented in the academic literature. Appraisal's problems of inaccuracy and inconsistency are so commonplace that social scientists have created an entire lexicon to describe the various categories of rater errors, biases, and tendencies that undermine its accuracy.
—Coens and Jenkins, *Abolishing Performance Appraisals*, p. 56

The rating scale is the most universal characteristic of all performance appraisals. These ratings are the source of much negativity and a host of bad memories. There is not much positive to report about ratings in appraisals. They are most often used to distinguish between the performance of one employee as compared to another for the chief purpose of making administrative decisions such as merit pay, recognition, and promotion. If this is the major reason to use ratings, then the cost may outweigh the benefit. There are a number of methods to make such decisions without the negative consequences associated with their use and the questions of their accuracy.

Judgment = Evaluation = Rating

Employees want feedback, not ratings, so employees will inevitably concentrate on their grade, not their feedback. This is consistent with the old adage regarding schoolchildren and their grades, "I *earned* an *A*, but I was *given* an *F!*" Our perception about positive and negative feedback is different, and a grade represents the worst form of feedback. Clearly, grading or rating performance is not neutral feedback, it is evaluative feedback.

The conventional approach, unless handled with consummate skill and delicacy, constitutes something dangerously close to a violation of the integrity of the personality. Managers are uncomfortable when they are put in the position of "playing God." The respect we hold for the inherent value of the individual leaves us distressed when we must take responsibility for judging the personal worth of a fellow man. Yet, the conventional approach to performance appraisal forces us not only to make such judgments and to see them acted upon but also to communicate them to those we have judged. Small wonder we resist!

—McGregor, "An Uneasy Look at Performance Appraisal," p. 3

After decades of rating, we are still attempting to make a bad process legitimate. Just trust me on this one, rating performance is simply a bad idea and a waste of your time.

Olympic Judges—or Why Rating Performance Is Not That Simple

In many Olympic sports, athletic performances are judged by a panel of experts. It is an amazing thing that the best judges in the world all look at the same performance at the same time and make different assessments; this is good commentary on the overall use of rating systems. It is a proven fact that qualitative performance criteria will vary, based on who is observing the performance.

In other Olympic sports, when there is an exact measurement or quantitative method to judge performance, it would simply appear that the first to cross the finish line is the best in the sport. However, the variations of mere hundreths of a second could be attributable to other factors. Could there be environmental, systemic, or personnel factors that made the difference in the athletes' performance?

Is it possible that a pair of Nike® shoes (equipment) as compared to a no-name brand shoe makes a .001 of a second difference? This could be the winning margin for a sprinter. Athletes report that certain lanes are easier to run on because of the curve of the track (environment). Two accomplished runners (coworkers) side-by-side may propel one another to their best performance as they are challenged by the other's ability and competitiveness. Could the .001 of a second be attributable to the coach (supervisor)?

Performance is a human phenomenon and it is not as quantitative as it may appear. Rating systems that assume that human factors can be reduced to simple numbers are incapable of managing performance. Finally, do all judges rate performance exactly as they see it each time? In a tale of international politics during the last few Summer Olympic Games, many have accused some judges of rating their countrymen higher than others.

It is a proven fact that qualitative performance criteria will vary, based on who is observing the performance.

Politics and Ratings

Aristotle remarked that "man is a political animal." To expect anything else goes against the nature of man. If this is so, then the accuracy of performance ratings will always be manipulated. Supervisors give employees ratings that are not based upon their performance alone for a number of human reasons.

> In fact, managers readily admit that their ratings often do not reflect actual employee performance. A majority (seventy percent) indicate that they inflate appraisal scores for the following reasons: to avoid deflating motivation, to enhance merit chances, to avoid exposing departmental problems, to avoid creating a negative personnel file, to protect good employees with personal problems, to reward great effort, to avoid confrontation, or to promote someone up and out. The same percentage (seventy percent) of managers also say they deflate scores to scare and employee into better performance, to punish a difficult employee, to encourage someone to quit, to create a file for dismissal, to minimize merit, or to comply with a higher directive discouraging high rating. (Longnecker et.al., 1987)
> —Glover, "Why Are We Ignoring Performance Appraisal Research?" p. 3

Accurate ratings are impossible when external factors overshadow the actual recording of performance events.

Dirty Dozen (Twelve More Reasons Why Ratings Don't Work)

If you still insist on more reasons why ratings do not work, here is a summary of a dozen more:

1. Ratings are past oriented—The goals of performance management are to maintain good performance, correct current performance, and improve future performance.

2. What is measured is not always what is rated—Many instruments are designed with seven to ten indices that do not reflect the actual content of the position or the expertise of the individual employee.

3. Describing and measuring what is "good" is often difficult to define within the constraints of an appraisal form. What is considered "good" varies greatly.

4. Supervisors do not always keep accurate records of performance, and therefore generalize good and bad performance. Most appraisals use a sample of performance, highlighting the major events and problem events, but ignoring consistent, positive performance over time.

5.   Rater biases are well documented. There are almost a dozen known phenomena that prove supervisors tend to rate employees inaccurately because of subconscious tendencies.

6.   Ratings are commonly based upon the supervisor's assessment alone. Employees have information that the supervisor does not and are present one hundred percent of the time. Therefore, employees need input into the performance management process.

7.   Ratings are often inflated—conflict avoidance or encouragement for poor performers are among the many reasons why ratings are inflated.

8.   Raters may rate some higher or lower than others for the same performance. What is "good" not only varies by who is rating the performance, but also by the employee being rated.

9.   Misuse of the idea that *nobody is perfect*. Managers feel an obligation to rate some employees lower so that it appears that they are properly supervising by identifying areas of improvement, even when it is not warranted.

10.   Not all work activities that are important are found on ratings scales.

11.   Different jobs often require different rating scales.

12.   Rating scales sometimes do not include behavioral factors, which are often as important as performance indices.

Rating systems are inconsistent with the true goals of performance management and undermine their potential effectiveness.

Rating systems are inconsistent with the true goals of performance management and undermine their potential effectiveness.

Ratings Block Discussion and Can Cause Emotional Harm

Employees eagerly or dreadfully anticipate their *grade*. The focus on the grade moves the attention from the Performance Review content to the grade. When the grade is not good (which is very subjective based upon the employee's definition of "good"), employees stop listening and in many circumstances performance suffers. "It leaves people bitter, crushed, bruised, battered, desolate, despondent, dejected, feeling inferior, some even depressed, unfit for work for weeks after receipt of rating, unable to comprehend why they are inferior" (Deming, 1986, p. 102).

A Good Rating Can Produce a Negative Response

As ratings are subject to the interpretation of the employee, a common occurrence is that a very good performer is dejected after receiving what the supervisor perceives to be a solid rating. A superstar performer who is given an A rating, but expected an A-plus rating, feels slighted. An employee who receives an excellent overall rating, but is marked down in a particular category, might disagree with the supervisor's assessment and react negatively. If a supervisor's good rating and an employee's expected rating vary greatly, it is problematic for both supervisor and employee.

Poor performers do not usually agree with their low ranking. The rating becomes a lightning rod for disagreement and heated discussion. Supervisors have to justify their ratings, thereby shifting dialogue from steps for improvement to examples that justify the rating. The conversation rarely produces any positive outcome, and both the supervisor and the employee feel "beat up" from the exchange.

Relationships Matter

Several authors note that some managers are reluctant to give employees critical feedback for fear that it will harm the relationship and their future ability to work with that person. It is confusing for the manager to be both a coach and a judge; employees have difficulty reconciling these contradictory roles as well. Organizations cannot build supportive relationships with their employees and empower them to take a more active role within the organization if employees are being rated.

> Even when a review is positive and the news is all good, an atmosphere of judgment continues to do damage. Introducing a judgmental attitude severely inhibits their relationship. When one person evaluates another, there's little possibility that either can be open. Small wonder that studies repeatedly find no correlation exists between productivity and Performance Reviews.
> —Farson and Keyes, *The Innovation Paradox*, p. 2002

Employees want feedback delivered in a coaching fashion with clear improvement plans. If the element of judgment is removed, it is more likely that the relationship can move closer to being a partnership with improved performance.

Employees want feedback delivered in a coaching fashion
with clear improvement plans.

Am I Compared Against a Standard or Against Others?

One of the chief problems with ratings is that the standard is not always clear. Is the employee evaluated against a previously defined standard or in comparison to others who perform similar work? How is a rookie employee judged fairly in a team of veterans who are all high performers? Is the rookie rated according to a defined standard or is he expected to attain the performance of the veterans?

What if the rookie was extremely talented and as a new employee outperformed the veterans? Should the rookie's high performance become the new standard? If pay or other administrative decisions are then tied to these ratings, the matter will become more complicated. Would we compensate a high performing rookie at the same level as veteran employees? Doing so might discount the veterans' years of service and loyalty to the company; not doing so would contradict the statement that we pay for performance. Few will regard either decision as fair.

Hemingway or Cave Man—How Well My Supervisor Communicates Affects Me

The manager's ability to communicate in writing can help or hinder an employee's performance reputation. Assuming an employee is a good performer, a manager who writes well can make good performance sound glorious and meritorious. In contrast, a manager who does not have good written communication skills can unintentionally devalue and dilute a good employee's official performance record.

Performance Appraisal Phrase Books

The fact that many managers resort to buying books to look for words or phrases to describe performance is evidence that they are not truly documenting actual performance; they are just creating an acceptable document. The success of these books shows that managers have so much trouble tracking, describing, recording, and rating performance in traditional performance appraisal systems that they need help. Phrase books are an affront to employees and their performance. The accuracy of the appraisal is absolutely in question when it is more reflective of an off-the-shelf book than it is of their manager's observations.

The primary goal of a performance discussion should be to describe accurately all aspects of performance. The second goal of the discussion should be to agree on the success criteria.

Information, Analysis, and Interpretation Should Be the Goals

The primary goal of a performance discussion should be to describe accurately all aspects of performance. The second goal of the discussion should be to agree on the success criteria. This allows the discussions to focus on generating information that is useful for managing performance, not creating a basis upon which to determine the value of contributions or to make administrative decisions. Ratings will never correct performance issues, but the performance information contained within them can be valuable. One could remove the rating from the performance management process and share only the information from which a rating could be built. This is exactly the approach taken within the Performance Conversations® model.

Solution: Abandon the use of ratings, and emphasize description, diagnosis, and discussion instead.

Eliminating quantitative ratings makes an incredible difference in the climate of any discussion about performance. It is the key to constructive discussions about work accomplishments.

—Drake, *Performance Appraisals*, p. 46

Ratings do not work. Ratings do not work. Ratings do not work. It is what it is. Organizations would be wise just to accept the fact. There is no evidence in the management literature that specifically links the use of ratings to improved performance. However, there is much written about the negative effects of being rated. If the aim is to provide feedback, ratings are unnecessary to describe or analyze performance, and are not beneficial in correcting poor performance, sustaining good performance, or improving performance. Performance management should emphasize description, analysis, and discussion and should avoid any form of "evaluation" of performance.

Performance improvement can only be achieved through a partnership with the employee. Together you can diagnose performance anomalies and create plans to continue that which is going well and to correct that which needs your collective attention. If the goal is to make administrative decisions, the accuracy of ratings is questionable. It is, therefore, a poor decision tool. Ratings are deemed worthless and damaging in performance management; managers should avoid their use.

Performance Conversations® Building Blocks

The Performance Conversations® model avoids the pitfalls of Fallacy F by avoiding the use of ratings since they have proven to be counterproductive and unnecessary for good performance management. Instead, **Progress Reviews** are used to discuss work, describe good and bad performance outcomes, analyze and characterize performance generally, and plan for future efforts. Traditional appraisals misplace their emphasis on past things that cannot be changed.

Scenario G – Only If Required

Performance Confrontations (Traditional Appraisals)

Manager: *Damion, come on in. I would like to talk to you. How are you today?*
Employee: *I'm okay. Did I do something wrong?*
Manager: *No, it is time for your annual review.*
Employee: *Oh!*
Manager: *I know this is sudden, but here it is. Read it and let me know if you have any questions.*
Employee: *I guess it is okay. Is the number at the bottom my final score?*
Manager: *Yes, it is. But it does not really matter. Your raise is only loosely tied to this form. We will decide what your raise will be in the fall before January increases are due.*
Employee: *That's a really good score, so I should get a good raise, but I'd like to know how I can earn the top scores from you each year.*
Manager: *Okay, we can talk about what we can do at a later time, but we need to complete the form today since they are due in to HR tomorrow.*

Performance Conversations®

Manager: *Damion, we have had a number of informal conversations over the recent weeks. This is a chance for us to sit down and take a bigger picture view of how things are going* [**Progress Review**]. *How do you think things are going?*
Employee: *I feel good about things. You and I've been in constant contact and I always feel like I know where I stand with you. If I do something good, you tell me. If there are problems, you tell me about those as well. So, I'm not sure why we need to sit down and talk about these things more.*
Manager: *Well, for two reasons. One, you might have feedback for me. Such as things that you need from me to do your job better. Or two, it is a chance for us to discuss any problems that might occur and notice good and bad patterns about work.*
Employee: *Oh.*
Manager: *An example is, have you noticed that I always call your attention to your paperwork, but never your work?*
Employee: *Not really.*

Manager: *This is exactly why it is important for us to stop working for a moment and notice what is going on around us. Your work is excellent, but you don't spend enough time on your administrative duties. Your reports get rolled up into department reports and then they are sent on to the corporate office for divisional reports. So, they are important. The biggest trend I've noticed is that you wait until the last minute to do your reports; this sometimes leads to inaccuracies.*

Employee: *You are probably right.*

Manager: *Is there anything I can do to help you get your paperwork done earlier and more accurately?*

Good supervision is far superior to traditional appraisals. The Performance Conversations® model incorporates supervision tools into its operations and works in context with other organizational efforts to manage performance. It includes both formal and informal performance management techniques, but the primary technique is feedback given and received in an atmosphere of support and partnership.

Fallacy G

Fallacy G: Performance appraisals are a necessary evil.

Truth: Many well-run organizations do not have a formal method of performance appraisal.

Scores of organizations in retail, finance, healthcare, utility, manufacturing, service, education industries and the public sector have done very well even though they have not given out report cards to their employees for many years.

—Coens, "Say Goodbye to Performance Appraisals (Really!) and Hello to a Happier, More Productive Workplace," p. 7

Why do performance appraisals? Performance appraisals are not a necessary evil. Since many successful organizations do not have a formal performance appraisal system, this should be compelling evidence that they are not always necessary for effective management. Performance appraisals are a part of a larger system that manages performance, so in the absence of a formal system of appraisal there are still other mechanisms that ensure the work is completed well.

Since many successful organizations do not have a formal performance appraisal system, this should be compelling evidence that they are not always necessary for effective management.

Informal Feedback Can Accomplish Most Objectives of Performance Management

A supervisor that makes frequent contact with subordinates, makes appropriate suggestions and corrections, holds impromptu discussions, meets with employees on a periodic basis, and seeks input from employees is accomplishing the vast majority of the goals of any performance management system. Perhaps the only elements that are missing in this scenario are the goals of documenting performance and the misplaced administrative desire to rate performance. Informal systems must exist whether formal systems exist or not, but not vice versa. Formal systems of appraisal are futile without informal systems of feedback.

Informal systems are effective at managing performance as evidenced by many successful organizations that do not have performance evaluations. One successful corporation often touted for its unique work environment and phenomenal success is the SAS Corporation of North Carolina. They are also noteworthy in that the organization has attained a high level of performance without the use of performance appraisals.

> Rather than emphasize pay, SAS has achieved an unbelievably low turnover rate [of] four percent —in an industry where the norm is closer to twenty percent—by offering intellectually engaging work; a family-friendly environment that features exceptional benefits; and an opportunity to work with fun, interesting people using state-of-the-art equipment.
> —Pfeffer-Stanford, "Six Dangerous Myths about Pay," p. 3

This reinforces the principle that the culture, environment, and quality of the work experience are more important performance drivers than a misdirected performance measurement or appraisal system.

Why Are Performance Appraisals Systems Always "New"?

Organizations are recognizing that performance appraisals are not driving the desired results. However, rather than accepting the compelling evidence against the use of performance appraisal, they assume it to be a flaw in their current tool. There is always a newer, smarter, and better performance appraisal system being considered or implemented.

Organizations tend to change their forms every three to five years, hoping that a new form will solve their problems. Not unsurprisingly, the form is the answer. Almost every organization attempts to evaluate performance—but few *really acknowledge* the failure of the process.

—Robinson, *How to Conduct Employees Performance Appraisals*, p. 4

Performance appraisals are not a necessary evil, they are just evil.

Are Results Feedback or Appraisal?

Many organizations have the ability to measure performance through purely quantitative methods such as sales results, quantity of widgets produced, or the number of customers assisted per hour. It is seemingly clear whether or not an individual has met the defined benchmark. It can be argued whether easily quantifiable results are feedback mechanisms or defacto evaluation devices. If only everything were as simple as the number of transactions completed. However, there is almost always room for qualitative judgments in most activities.

Gallant efforts that produce marginal results complicate
the use of results as the sole measure of appraisals.

If results are feedback devices, then results can be used in a larger context *along with other information* to manage performance and behavior. If results are evaluative devices, then additional and separate appraisal activity may not be needed, but other performance activities could be ignored or deemphasized inadvertently. An obvious omission in the use of results is behavior. Here are some examples: a salesman may be successful with clients but has an attitude that may offend peers; a widget producer may consistently arrive late but can still meet the numerical quotas for production; a customer service representative may lack cultural sensitivities that are important for the company to enter new markets; and a manager may have a productive unit but his poor treatment of staff members causes constant turnover.

Gallant efforts that produce marginal results complicate the use of results as the sole measure of appraisals. Results and outcomes are the best feedback mechanisms for performance, but they are not sufficient alone to manage performance.

A Poor System Is Worse than No System

A poor system or an unused good system can have an equally damaging effect on morale as employees will undoubtedly see the weaknesses of both systems. At least when there is no formal appraisal system, there are always other informal mechanisms in place to manage performance. Sound advice for managers would be: if there is a system in place, use it effectively. Otherwise, the haphazard use of a good system will send conflicting messages to employees about the importance of performance and productivity.

Solution: Do not use traditional performance appraisals.

Organizations can avoid performance appraisal systems altogether by having other informal and formal organization elements that manage performance. These include solid HR policies, well trained managers, a supportive culture, and self-directed teams, or other empowerment-based systems. Some alternate methods of performance management include full performance systems without rating or grading, programs that are not tied to pay and rewards, coaching systems, narrative forms of performance management, individual development plans, some forms of Critical Incident method, and the Performance Conversations® model.

Performance Conversations® Building Blocks

Fallacy G advises that organizations avoid appraisal, the Performance Conversations® model is an alternative to appraisal and is what to do in place of them. The model is superior to traditional appraisal as its foundational elements are good supervision and frequent feedback. These two elements are necessary for proper management in any circumstance, as opposed to appraisals which are not necessary for good performance.

Scenario H – You Are Picking On Me

Performance Confrontation (Traditional Appraisal)

Manager: *Claire, I'm going to document the things that we talked about today for the file because they are so important. I want to make sure that I've been clear about all of the things that I expect of you in the coming weeks.*

Employee: *It feels like you are picking on me. You don't have these kinds of conversations with anyone else in the department, and when you meet with others you don't document those conversations for the file. I know, I asked others and you never do.*

Manager: *I don't have a file on everyone else because everyone else is doing a good job.*

Employee: *So, the only reason you have a file on me is because you are trying to discipline me. You never liked me, so you are waiting for me to make a mistake so that you can fire me.*

Manager: *I'm sorry that you feel that way.*

Employee: *No, I think that you think that I'm sorry, a poor performer. You have never treated me fairly. Ever since I made that one mistake two years ago, it is as if I can't do anything right in your eyes.*

Performance Conversations®

Manager: *Claire, what do you make of all this information that you and I've collected in your Performance Portfolio?*

Employee: *I'm not sure what to make of it.*

Manager: *It is kind of sobering, don't you think?*

Employee: *What do you mean?*

Manager: *There is a lot of information here, but it is not balanced. There is not enough information here to show that you are succeeding. There is too much information about challenges, concerns, and other distractions from the work that I know you are capable of doing.*

Employee: *I'm not sure that it contains all the right information. It does not contain all of the good stuff I do as well.*

Manager: *I'm sure that you are right. It shows that most of the stuff in here is information that I collected or information from company reports. But, you do know that we both own this Performance Portfolio? We both are supposed to put in the good stuff, the not-so-good stuff, and any other information that we can find that tells the story of how you are doing. Do you have documents or other evidence that should be added?*

Employee: *Not right off hand I don't.*

Manager: *How about your Performance Log? Have you been keeping it up?*

Employee: *Yes, I have.*

Manager: *Well, let's talk about information that you have tracked that would show a different picture about how well you are performing!*

Employee: *Ahh, it is not as up-to-date as it could be.*

Manager: (sits silently)

Employee: *I guess all of this means that I've not been doing as well as I could or should have been doing?*

Because Performance Conversations® are based upon evidence instead of memories, it is a better way of tracking and managing performance than traditional appraisal techniques. It is even more powerful that the employee has responsibility for showing how things are going and for justifying that they are doing the things that are expected. Since all of the evidence about performance is always available, the employee always knows how he or she is doing. The burden of proof needed to justify corrections, discipline, terminations, recognition, or promotions is ready made and always available for both the employee and the manager to view.

Fallacy H

Fallacy H: Appraisals are necessary for documentation and administrative decisions

Truth: Appraisals and documentation are not the same thing

Except where appraisals are contractually promised to employees, appraisals are not required for legal documentation. Appraisal evidence also is not particularly helpful in defending lawsuits. In fact, appraisal evidence helps employees at least as much as is does employers in the litigation of wrongful discharge and discrimination claims. Counseling memoranda and other documentation will work better because they are specific to the problem and more timely.

—Coens, "Say Goodbye to Performance Appraisals (Really!) and Hello to a Happier, More Productive Workplace," p. 6

Appraisals and Administrative Decisions

The use of appraisal ratings is often defended by the need to justify raises, promotions, and demotions, yet appraisal instruments are only one potential source of performance data. Results and other outcomes are usually more important than the numbers on a performance appraisal instrument. Also, appraisals commonly do not contain behavioral dimensions. Yet, it is behavior that creates results, policy violations, illegal activities, revenues, efforts, teamwork, and countless other indicators that should be documented. Conducting appraisals only to create documentation for administrative decisions is misguided because such tools rarely contain all performance related information.

Appraisals commonly do not contain behavioral dimensions.

Appraisals and Organizational Decision-Making

Managers ultimately make personnel decisions based upon a number of factors, such as organizational need, fairness, and seniority. Efforts, behaviors, outcomes, and results are all important factors seldom accounted for on most appraisal instruments. One employee may be better at a particular function, but his coworker is better at a function that is more critical to the organization's mission. Organizations should face the reality that performance appraisal instruments do not account for all considerations, yet they are used as a primary tool for managing and rewarding employees.

Managers ultimately make personnel decisions based upon a number of factors such as organizational need, fairness, and seniority. Organizations should face the reality that performance appraisal instruments do not account for all considerations, yet they are used as a primary tool for managing and rewarding employees.

It is harder to justify why an employee with a good rating was not promoted. Managers want the flexibility to make tough situational decisions; appraisals hinder this freedom. A number of court cases highlight this exact dilemma: an employee with an excellent evaluation asks the organization to justify why he or she was not promoted. There are also circumstances when poorly completed performance evaluations actually help the plaintiff-employee more so than the defendant-employer because the inconsistent rating pattern demonstrates inconsistent and unfair supervision.

Pay Decisions Are Not Made by Appraisal Alone

There are a number of factors that affect pay. Therefore, creating the expectation that only the appraisal results will govern employee pay is misleading.

> The salary that an employee commands conforms to a variety of social and personal facts. The use of performance appraisals as a basis for salary changes concentrates only on the perception of the employee's performance, disregarding all the other facts. Among the factors affecting an individual's salary are: market rate, responsibilities, skills, education, prosperity of the company and the community, seniority, individual performance, and all other personality traits. The complex combination of these facts determines what the employee will be paid.
> —Allender, "Reengineering Employee Performance Appraisals the TQM Way," p. 3

Many organizations link pay to the appraisal process, but then limit merit increases based on where an individual falls within their current pay range. Similarly, some organizations stop providing increases to employees who have achieved the maximum pay rate for their job classification, or they do not provide incentive pay in challenging economic times. The organization's compensation and performance management practices have different goals. When they are not coordinated, they send mixed signals to employees about what is expected and what is valued. It is problematic to tie pay to the performance management process.

Many organizations link pay to the appraisal process, but then limit merit increases based on where an individual falls within their current pay range. The organization's compensation and performance management practices have different goals. When they are not coordinated, they send mixed signals.

Documentation, Discipline, and Regulatory Requirements

The documentation necessary to justify that employees are managed fairly can come in many forms. A record of results, letters of appreciation or reprimand, a supervisor's journal, records of critical incidents, the presence or absence of differential pay over time, the presence or absence of recognition devices and rewards, departmental performance data, feedback from customers and peers, reports, work samples and other miscellaneous data can be used to explain how an individual's performance or behavior compares to that of their coworkers. The best documentation of poor performance is letters written during the progressive discipline process as they are specific to the issue. If properly prepared, these letters note all the pertinent information necessary to satisfy external agencies. There is no specific legislation or regulatory requirement that prescribes what type of documentation is required, and certainly there is no legal requirement for documenting performance with appraisal instruments.

It is a prudent activity to keep records of performance events. However, it is not necessary to use this documentation to form value judgments (appraise) nor to make administrative decisions. Records generated to provide information about performance are valuable as a basis for analyzing and understanding performance. No information should be used in isolation of other pertinent data to make important administrative decisions.

He Who Has the Most Documentation *Should* Win—In Court

Supervisors who wish to terminate employees or justify discipline are usually conscientious about documenting performance deficiencies. However, there are times when complete documentation of an employee's shortcomings backfires in court. If the employee's attorney asks the supervisor to produce evidence of good or neutral performance, it is problematic for most managers. So, if the plaintiff's attorney can prove even a single occasion when the employee performed well, it might undermine the manager's poor performance documentation. Single-sided documentation supports the plaintiff's allegation that the employee was singled out and treated unfairly by the manager and that the plaintiff's flaws are no better or worse than their coworkers. Record keeping should be rigorous, but balanced, to include good, poor, and neutral performance indicators.

Supervisors also do a disservice to the performance management process when they haphazardly complete appraisals or inflate ratings. This older written evidence from the supervisor can contradict the supervisor's recent account of the employee's poor performance. Positive ratings for marginal employees point to the supervisor being incompetent, biased, or careless when he or she attempts to discipline or terminate an employee for a specific infraction.

Solution: Other management systems can be used to document performance and meet administrative requirements.

There are a number of elements and a variety of data necessary to manage performance, and all sources should be considered in making administrative decisions. Managers should be trained to track and account for good, bad, and neutral performance on an ongoing basis. Nonetheless, a better approach to supervision would be to get the employee involved in keeping records and tracking and monitoring their own performance. This creates instant feedback for the employee and creates a better working relationship with the supervisor. The Performance Conversations® model provides a method of tracking and documenting performance.

Performance Conversations® Building Blocks

Through the use of **Performance Logs** and **Performance Portfolios**, the Performance Conversations® model improves documentation and incorporates the solution to Fallacy *H*. Far better than the goal of collecting information for punitive purposes, the Performance Conversations® approach gathers as much information as possible in order to fully understand the work that is being performed. This data informs decision making about how to plan for and execute future work. Employees are also empowered by the information they helped to collect because they always know how they are doing. The **Performance Log** and **Performance Portfolio** collected by the manager and employee are a balanced scorecard type approach to performance management.

Summary of False Assumptions

Employees are intrinsically motivated. When we use twenty-first-century thinking, we stop trying to buy our employees' attention, to trick them into being interested in management initiatives, to manipulate them with an assortment of carrots, or to threaten them with a variety of sticks. External sources of motivation are not necessary because employees generally want to succeed and do good work for their organization. So, the work of top management should be to create an environment in which natural human potential is nourished and unleashed.

The false assumption that employees can be manipulated like other variables within the organization has led us to create paternalistic, autocratic, and bureaucratic systems to exert control. But people are complex and will never respond to incentives like machines or animals. Evaluation-based performance appraisals are old human resource management technology that convey the message that employees are expendable parts of a system; and if they do not get an acceptable rating, they need to be repaired or replaced. Furthermore, where is the evidence the ratings are effective as a motivational device? By contrast, there is considerable research and empirical evidence supporting the idea that motivation is intrinsic and that employees are motivated by challenge, responsibility, and a positive work environment.

People want feedback, not appraisals; they want conversations and dialogue, not ratings and evaluations. People seek dignity and pride in their work, not criticism and oversight. The late great management guru, Peter Drucker, is said to have remarked that we should "treat our subordinates as if they were all volunteers" as our approach to management in the twenty-first century. This is a useful metaphor for managers to consider and one of the guiding frameworks for this book. After all, employees volunteer their commitment—commitment is not something that can be compelled.

Evaluation-based performance appraisals are old human resource management technology that conveys the message that employees are expendable parts of a system; and if they do not get an acceptable rating, they need to be repaired or replaced.

Fallacies, Truths, and Solutions—A Listing of False Assumptions

Fallacy E: Appropriately designed incentives will motivate employees to perform better.

Truth: Motivation is intrinsic—Extrinsic motivation has very limited effectiveness.

Solution: Providing challenging, meaningful work; creating a nurturing and supportive environment; and involving employees in decisions that affect their work—these imperatives encourage pride in workmanship and personal growth. This is the key to sustained motivation.

Fallacy F: Rating (or grading) performance is sound management.

Truth: Ratings reflect Theory X management.

Solution: Abandon the use of ratings, and emphasize description, diagnosis, and discussion instead.

Fallacy G: Performance appraisals are a necessary evil.

Truth: Many well-run organizations do not have a formal method of performance appraisal.

Solution: Do not use traditional performance appraisals.

Fallacy H: Appraisals are necessary for documentation and administrative decisions.

Truth: Appraisals and documentation are not one and the same thing.

Solution: Other management systems can be used to document performance and meet administrative requirements.

Quick Reference Points

Chapter 5

- Incentives work a small amount and only in the short term.

- There are significant negative side effects with the use of incentives.

- Motivation is intrinsic.

- People are motivated by good work and a great work environment.

- People want challenge and responsibility, achievement and trust.

- Ratings cause fear and discontentment in the workplace.

- No one has ever designed a rating system that is completely accurate or fair.

- Managers manipulate ratings for a variety of reasons, and therefore render them useless.

- Ratings destroy working relationships.

- Many successful organizations do not have performance appraisal systems.

- Good supervision and informal feedback systems meet all of the objectives of performance management systems without the negative aftertaste of appraisals.

- There are dozens of ways to document performance, and appraisals are some of the most inaccurate and incomplete methods available.

Chapter 6

Human Fallacies

It is stated that all systems can break down at the human level. For performance appraisals, this is painfully true. While we can count on machines to operate the way they were designed all of the time, human behavior is less predictable, less reliable, and not foolproof, all major reasons why performance appraisal systems do not work as intended. Traditional models of appraisal may actually inhibit effective performance because of the belief that the supervisor can see and know all. Therefore, any system built on this notion is doomed to fail, even before it is implemented.

Performance is an art. People do not wake each morning, arrive at work each day, and perform in the exact same manner that they did the day before. Employees are not able to perform perfectly each and every time. It is a fallacy to assume that human behavior is so regimented and predictable.

Performance appraisal sessions are commonly emotional events. Inherently, many managers are uncomfortable with the prospect of judging or evaluating others. Instinctively, employees are uncomfortable being the recipient of such judgments. As a result, tensions rise, emotions boil, and words often become heated even before any real feedback is shared.

Surprisingly, in the typical performance appraisal process, managers are not expected to bring any of their humanity into the session. These systems assume that managers are totally objective and that they can, and do, make accurate decisions without error or bias. The designers of these systems argue that training can overcome basic human tendencies. Often managers are not even trained effectively to supervise, much less to conduct a Performance Review session.

In addition to general fallacies and false assumptions, human limitations undermine the prospect that performance appraisals can be effective management tools. Three fallacies of human behavior in the context of performance appraisals are discussed in this chapter.

Fallacy I: Supervisors are omniscient; they see and know all.

Fallacy J: A well-trained supervisor can overcome rater bias.

Fallacy K: Supervisors and employees see value in performance appraisals.

Scenario I — Do You See What I See?

Performance Confrontation (Traditional Appraisals)

Manager: *Robert, I continue to be concerned about how you close sales. It seems that you are a bit reluctant to close strongly and ask the customer to buy our products at the end of your calls.*

Employee: *What do you mean?*

Manager: *When I listen to you speak to customers, I notice that you handle the call well except for ending with phrases like, "Can I place an order for you today?" or "Should I send you a dozen or a case of our new model"?*

Employee: *I usually ask the customer for an order at the end of a call, just like we learned in training.*

Manager: *But I've heard you on more than one occasion fail to do so!*

Employee: *I'm sure that I ask the customer 95 percent of the time. So, I'm not sure when you are listening in. The only time that I recall not asking a customer is when the customer has stated more than once that they are not interested in buying, and I've tried to overcome their objection more than once.*

Manager: *I don't want to argue about this. I just want you to follow procedures.*

Employee: *Even if I did not do it when you were checking me that doesn't mean that I don't do it most of the time. My sales numbers are better than most other representatives, so I must be doing something right!*

Performance Conversations®

Manager: *All the evidence in our Performance Portfolio shows that you are doing better than most representatives.*

Employee: *I'm trying hard to make every sale I can.*

Manager: *That's great. The results speak for themselves. But, on at least two occasions, I've heard you miss a cue and not try to close the sale with a customer you were on the phone with.*

Employee: *That's surprising. I always close with a request for an order. At least, the times when I don't are when I've already tried to make the sale earlier and the cus-*

tomer has said no more than once. In those situations, I don't end the call abruptly, I continue to describe other products or see if the customer has any additional questions. I've found that some of them call back a week or two later if you don't put too much pressure on them on the initial call.

Manager: *That makes sense. I just wanted to make sure that you were following procedures, but it sounds like you know what to do and when to do it.*

Employee: *I'm trying.*

Manager: *Great. I'm going to update my Performance Log to note that you are doing a good job of asking for and closing sales and that you use good judgment in how you relate to customers!*

Employee: *Thank you. I'm glad you noticed.*

Performance Conversations are better than traditional appraisals because they rely on numerous examples of performance gathered by both the employee and manager and recorded in Performance Logs and the Performance Portfolio. This documented evidence stands in contrast to a few samples of performance noticed by the manager only. The risk is that a sampling of performance may give a skewed view of what is actually happening. The employee has a perspective that is different than the supervisor, and this information must be used to give a complete picture of performance.

Fallacy I

Fallacy I: Supervisors are omniscient; they see and know all.

Truth: Supervisors do not see everything, miss some things, and often take vacations.

Better supervisors will improve performance, but even better supervisors will not eliminate the limitations and shortcomings of performance appraisal systems that rely on the supervisor's observations only.

Supervisors Are Humans

Despite the idyllic vision of an all-powerful and infallible supervisor with a large *S* on his chest, the sad truth is that supervisors are human. Supervisors are not superheroes. Supervisors make mistakes and when mistakes are made in supervising employees, the implications are great. Yet, in the use of performance appraisals, supervisor mistakes or inadequacies are not documented, while the employee's shortcomings are highlighted.

Sometimes, supervisors are unaware of workplace incidents, uninformed about details, and unable to respond in the appropriate way at any given point in time. These statements are not made to accuse all supervisors of being incompetent, but to argue that supervisors are human and thus do not do the right and best thing one hundred percent of the time. Perfection is simply not a human characteristic. Organizations must do a better job of hiring, training, and developing competent supervisors. Better supervisors will improve performance but even better supervisors will not eliminate the limitations and shortcomings of performance appraisal systems that rely on the supervisor's observations only.

Supervisors Take Vacations

One disadvantage that supervisors have in observing performance is that they are not always present. The employee is present one hundred percent of the time and is undoubtedly in a position to observe their own work behavior as well as, or better than, the supervisor. Therefore, the employee should be trained and expected to observe, track, monitor, and record elements of their own performance. An employee might even do her best work when the supervisor is not around because she must think and act without guidance. Supervisors who take breaks, take vacations, or who are working on tasks other than supervising are threats to effective performance appraisals as they are traditionally practiced.

Supervisors who take breaks, take vacations, or who are working on tasks other than supervising are threats to effective performance appraisals as they are traditionally practiced.

Supervisors Are Not Experts in Everything

The major task of a supervisor is to accomplish work through others, not to know the technical detail of each subordinate's job. Indeed, many management theorists claim that frontline supervisors know ninety percent of the content of their subordinate's jobs, middle managers know seventy percent, and senior managers know only thirty percent. Supervisors may know an even lower percentage of what their subordinates do when they have many different functional areas reporting to them. Because of this limited purview, it is not possible for supervisors to make absolute ratings about performance.

Do You See What I See? Employee May Know More Than Supervisor

> [E]mployees possess valid, unique, and relevant performance information
> and insight that is unavailable or unobservable by the rater.
> —Roberts, "Employee Performance Appraisal System Participation," p. 2

If the employee is properly trained, experienced, and takes the job seriously, it is likely that he or she understands the requirements of the job better than the supervisor. It is even a preferable scenario for the employee to be a genuine expert in her work. A good use of an employee's expertise is to be involved in the planning, implementation, and assessment of work.

> Someone external to a given job, such as a supervisor or a quality control
> inspector, frequently sets the standard for the job. However, standards can
> be written effectively by employees as well. Experienced employees usually
> know what constitutes satisfactory performance of tasks in their job descrip-
> tions, and so do their supervisors. Therefore, these individuals often can par-
> ticipate in setting standards with their managers.
> —Mathis and Jackson, *Human Resource Management*, p. 342

The employee can, and should, have a perspective that, when combined with their manager's view, creates a more complete picture of all work tasks and requirements.

A good use of an employee's expertise is to be involved in the planning, implementation, and assessment of work.

Solution: Train managers very well in the science of supervision and require employees to be highly involved in performance management process.

Supervisors are human and therefore are fallible. Because they make mistakes, take vacations, have bad days, forget things, and sometimes have other responsibilities, they cannot see all and know all regarding any subordinate's performance. Therefore, any performance management system that relies only on the supervisor's evaluation of subordinate's performance is fatally flawed.

The employees know a great deal about the work they perform and should be the first step in the performance management process. Supervisors who assume they know it all will insult their subordinates, will miss valuable performance data, and will make poor judgments based upon incomplete information. Engaged, empowered, and involved employees will know how to apply efforts, will learn to perform self-checks, will track progress against standards, and will critically evaluate outcomes in comparison to goals. Another benefit to this approach is when individuals are self-managed and self-directed, there is a greater pride in outcomes, and thus improved performance. The Performance Conversations® model employs this technique.

Performance Conversations® Building Blocks

Employee involvement is the antidote to Fallacy I. The Performance Conversations® model engages the employee in the design, delivery, and the management of their efforts through the *Performance Planning* process, in the keeping of the *Performance Log* and the *Performance Portfolio*, by their participation in *Progress Reviews*, and through their reflection during the *Annual Performance Analysis and Summary*. Traditional appraisals rely on the supervisor's observations alone. Such appraisals are shortsighted since employees are the primary source of information about what happens with their work. Performance Conversations® acknowledge the indispensable role of the employee in performance management.

Scenario J – Rater Errors

Performance Confrontations (Traditional Appraisals)

Manager: *Corlethea, your work continues to improve. You are doing well in every aspect of your job. I want to say thank you for your hard work and your extra work.*

Employee: *Good! I'm glad to be recognized for the work I do.*

Manager: *Do you have any questions about your evaluation?*

Employee: *I would like to know how I'm doing in comparison to others!*

Manager: *That's important, but our emphasis today should be on what you do. You do a good job, and as long as you are doing your best, your evaluation will reflect your outstanding efforts.*

Employee: *Thank you. But, how do I rank in comparison to other employees you supervise?*

Manager: *I'm not sure why this is important to you.*

Employee: *There are a lot of rumors out there that the men in the department get better treatment than the women.*

Manager: *Why would you say that?*

Employee: *It is just what I've heard. Sarah and Heather both say that you treat the guys better than the ladies, and that all of the guys get better evaluations.*

Manager: *That's certainly not true. Some of the guys are struggling right now, some have been disciplined, and some are doing well. I evaluate everyone fairly.*

Employee: *The rumor on the grapevine is the guys who go for drinks with you and the crowd every Friday after work somehow do better on evaluations, even though many of them are not good performers.*

Performance Conversations®

Manager: *Corlethea, your work continues to improve. You are doing well in every aspect of your job. I want to say thank you for your hard work and your extra work.*

Employee: *Good! I'm glad to be recognized for the work I do.*

Manager: *Do you have any questions about your evaluation?*

Employee: *I would like to know how I'm doing in comparison to others!*

Manager: *That's hard to say as everyone's performance has so many variables. But you are certainly doing better than most based upon the evidence that we have in your Performance Portfolio. I also hope that you know that you are doing well. We have talked about your good work at each of our last few Progress Reviews.*

Employee: *I think I know, but how do I rank in comparison to other employees you supervise? I've heard rumors that men are treated differently than women.*

Manager: *As you know, Corlethea, we don't rank employees at Virginia Technology Solutions. The evidence of their performance is in their **Performance Logs** and **Performance Portfolios**, just like yours. Their work samples, awards, thank you notes, reports, and information should show how they are doing. If the information is not in there, it would be hard to show that they are performing better than anyone else. I do acknowledge that I have good working relationships with some of the guys and some very good personal relationships with others, but their work is judged by the evidence.*

Employee: *I just wanted to make sure that I'm being treated fairly as compared to others.*

Manager: *I can assure you that you are. As a matter of fact, the best part of the Performance Conversations® approach is that the characterization of your work is not done by me alone. You also help to paint the picture of your performance by keeping your **Performance Log** and the **Performance Portfolio**. So, using those tools makes sure that the facts are balanced. Favoritism is hard to justify, as the facts will speak for themselves in the Performance Conversations® approach.*

By focusing on evidence that justifies the characterization of work and by involving the employee in their own evaluation, the potential for bias in Performance Conversations® is virtually eliminated. In contrast, traditional evaluations rely on the observation of the supervisor only and therefore they are susceptible to the naturally occurring bias that all humans possess.

Fallacy J

Fallacy J: A well-trained supervisor can overcome rater bias.

Truth: Most of us are human.

The best performance review system in the world easily can be brought to its knees by the way an individual manager delivers a review to an employee.
—Deblieux, *Performance Appraisal Source Book*, p. 27

Individual vs. System

It has been said that if we put good performers in bad systems, the systems will win every time.
—Ripley, "Improving Employee Performance," p. 1

At this point, there should be no question that performance appraisals do not work. Supervisors are often put into the impossible position of working with performance appraisal systems that damage ultimate performance, versus enhances it. Therefore, regardless of how well supervisors are trained, it may be impossible for supervisors to use adequately any of the most commonly used performance appraisal tools. Many systems expect the supervisor to overcome the very nature of being human. Not all human perceptions are accurate—this is just a reality that few designers of performance management systems seem to acknowledge.

Not all human perceptions are accurate—this is just a reality that few designers of performance management systems seem to acknowledge.

Rater Errors

The subject of rating errors has been heavily researched, and according to experts, supervisors usually rate performance incorrectly because of hidden biases. A review of rater errors noted by Noe, et. al. (2006) or Mathis and Jackson (2003) are as follows:

Similar to or Different From Me. Employees who are of a similar race, gender, religion, appearance, belief system, or background as the rater are often rated higher than those who are not.

Primacy and Recency Effect. Things that have happened toward the end of the rating period (most recent) or at the beginning of the rating period receive more attention.

Contrast. Individuals are compared against one another instead of to an agreed upon standard.

Leniency, Strictness and Central Tendency. Grades are either too easy, too strict, or everyone is rated the same.

Halo and Horns or *Good and Bad Impressions.* The employee makes one mistake and everything that follows will always be suspect, or the employee does one thing well and everything that follows is presumed to be good.

Sampling Error. Ratings are based upon only a few performance events, and all performance is assumed to be of the same quality.

The caveat in numerous management texts is that we are all biased, and the goal is for supervisors to be aware of their biases so that they can reduce their occurrence. There is no author that argues that rater errors can be completely overcome.

Training on the Performance Management Instrument

The scenario has been played out in organizations many times: supervisors crowd into a meeting room for a mandatory training session by HR to roll out the new performance appraisal process. Commonly, the system was designed for the organization by outside consultants. There is seldom one hundred percent attendance from supervisors who are "required" to use the system, and senior managers almost never participate. Newly hired or newly promoted managers likely miss the training altogether, but all supervisors are expected to use the system consistently across the organization. Training is almost always a one-shot deal, and there is seldom any follow-up to ensure that supervisors are properly using the system.

Supervisors Who Were Not Trained to Supervise

One assumption regarding performance management is that supervisors have mastered the basics of supervision. The most significant reason for failure of performance management systems is that supervisors do not properly supervise by giving employees sufficient feedback over time. This failure of basic supervision is only accentuated when the supervisor attempts to have the first meaningful performance conversation in a year with an employee during the annual performance appraisal. At this point, a year has passed, as have many opportunities for dialogue and improvement.

The most significant reason for failure of performance management systems is that supervisors do not properly supervise by giving employees sufficient feedback over time.

One Best-Way Method—My Way

One of the major biases that supervisors have is that, "My way is best." So, it is only natural that managers will perceive employees who take their suggestion and advice more positively than those who do things well, but who prefer to do things in a different manner. This viewpoint discounts the potential knowledge, ability, and intelligence of the subordinate. A better solution would be to have an environment that encourages the supervisor and subordinate to collaborate fully on the work and the success criteria. Getting employees involved in the planning, execution, monitoring, and quality control of their work is the best method for reaching peak performance.

Solution: Either hire androids, or abandon the use of rating systems and require employees to be involved in the tracking of their efforts.

Eliminating human bias is not possible. With the realization that everyone has bias, no matter how well intentioned, it would be wise to avoid systems that rely only on the supervisor's observations. The only way to prevent bias in ratings is to not do ratings. Instead organizations should create performance management systems that include the input of employees and other data to balance the bias of a supervisor.

Performance Conversations® Building Blocks

The Performance Conversations® model provides a balanced view of work as both the employee and supervisor contribute information to characterize the employee's performance. The dual **Performance Logs** and the shared **Performance Portfolio** provide enough evidence of performance to describe it well. Since the Performance Conversations® approach does not utilize a rating system, bias is mitigated as there is never a final judgment of performance. Instead, information is generated and used to solve problems, not to make administrative decisions.

Scenario K — Is It Something I Said?

Performance Confrontations (Traditional Appraisals)

Manager: *Lucy, you continue to do an excellent job on all of your work. The Hagersville Tire Company is proud to have you as a member of the staff.*

Employee: *Good, I love my job.*

Manager: *As you can see, you were rated as outstanding and have earned an almost perfect score.*

Employee: *Oh!*

Manager: *You did a noteworthy job on most things. You did great on A, B, C and D. The only area for potential improvement is E.*

Employee: *You don't like my work on E? I thought I did that well.*

Manager: *You do, but I know that you can do even better because . . . ! What's wrong? Did I say something to offend you?*

Employee: *I used to get all 5's. Since you have come to Hagersville, I cannot do anything right* (sniffling).

Manager: *I hope that you believe that you do everything near perfectly, but we all can improve on something. You have 5's on eight of the ten categories and a 4.9 overall.*

Employee: *I know but . . .*

Manager: *Why are you crying? This was supposed to be a good evaluation! You are a great person . . .*

Employee: *I don't feel so great; I feel more like a failure!*

Performance Conversations®

Manager: *Lucy, did you get a chance to review the Performance Logs and Performance Portfolio?*

Employee: *Yes, I did. It is filled with a lot of good information.*

Manager: *Yes, it is. What do you think about A, B, C, & D?*

Employee: *It appears that I did well on all of those.*

Manager: *You did! How about E?*

Employee: *Well, our records say that it is not my best work.*

Manager: *What can we do about E & F? I think that we need to make some adjustments!*

Employee: *I agree. How about we try . . .*

Using the Performance Conversations® approach eliminates the fear of something bad happening (getting a bad rating, not getting a raise, etc.). This creates a climate that cultivates open and honest discussions about work. Employees will more likely seek feedback when it is focused on performance improvement only, instead of data that will be used to form a judgment about performance for a rating or evaluation.

Fallacy K

People hate performance reviews. This would appear to be almost a universal law of modern business. Whether you call them evaluations, appraisals, counseling sessions, employees seem to have developed a great distaste for the ritual of having their yearly contribution summarized and categorized in one 90-minute meeting. Most managers dread giving this annual dose of medicine almost as much as employees dislike receiving it.

—Markle, *Catalytic Coaching*, p. 1

Many authors agree that employees and their supervisors dislike the performance appraisal process. It is no wonder that performance appraisals are ineffective. The sheer emotion and disregard expressed toward the process ensures that it will not be done well or well received. Appraisals spark an emotional reaction that is matched by few other things in the workplace. When people dislike something as much as they dislike appraisals, there is not much good that can come from the process. Organizations should recognize that these negative reactions are counterproductive to productivity.

The sheer emotion and disregard expressed toward the process ensures that it will not be done well or well received. Appraisals spark an emotional reaction that is matched by few other things in the workplace.

Fallacy K: Supervisors and employees see value in performance appraisals.

Truth: Rarely are kind words spoken about the performance appraisal process.

Superiors are profoundly uncomfortable rating people on performance, and they execute this important task poorly.

—*Harvard Business Review*, pp. 73–74

Dislike Leads to Delay and Avoidance

It is hard to do something well if one has negative feelings about completing the task. Supervisors avoid doing performance appraisals, fail to do them, or complete them ineffectively in order to avoid the conflict that comes when sitting in judgment of another person. The problem is not the supervisor or the employee, the problem is the system. Performance appraisal systems create a false adversarial relationship between the supervisor and employee. If there is an adversarial relationship between the supervisor and employee, it virtually guarantees that performance will suffer.

Judge Me Not

Managers and supervisors who must complete appraisals of their employees often resist the appraisal process. Many managers feel that their role calls on them to assist, encourage, coach, and counsel employees to improve their performance. However, being a judge on the one hand and a coach and counselor on the other may cause internal conflict and confusion for many managers.

—Mathis and Jackson, *Human Resource Management*, p. 363

Many managers do not like the role of judge for many reasons:

- It feels unnatural to serve in the role of a judge of those individuals with whom we share a relationship.

- Supervisors are seldom trained to "evaluate" others properly.

- Supervisors do not always have enough information to make good decisions.

- Employees are unwilling to accept the supervisor's perspective, and often challenge it.

Finally, it is simply difficult to sit across from someone and give critical feedback that could impact their career. While it is difficult to give negative feedback, it is even more difficult to provide negative conclusions—and ratings are nothing more than conclusions. Supervisors should be trained to be coaches, not judges.

Employees Hate Appraisals

Almost everyone complains about performance evaluations. Employees dislike them because they feel powerless getting a "report card" that is based on arbitrary, confusing, and biased factors.

—Robinson, *How to Conduct Employees Performance Appraisals*, p. A-1

Employees want feedback, not appraisal.

Parent and Child Relationship

> Most performance review systems reinforce a paternalistic world, one built on distrust and the assumption that the boss knows more about our skills, abilities, and commitment than we do. This dependency works against empowerment.
>
> —Maurer, *The Feedback Toolkit*, p. 51

Father knows best. Many performance management systems treat employees, regardless of their age, ability, knowledge, or length of service as if they are professional children. Some expect these professional children to wait for instructions and disposition from management. The supervisor assumes a position of unquestioned authority—it is also assumed that the subordinate is less capable than the supervisor. McGregor notes:

> The conventional approach, on the other hand, makes the assumption that the superior can know enough about the subordinate to decide what is best for him.
>
> —McGregor, "An Uneasy Look at Performance Appraisal," p. 5

Emotional Subject

> No one feels comfortable in threatening situations; usually we try to avoid them. PA is no exception. For most employees, fear is present even before the discussion begins. People dislike being judged—especially when the evaluation comes from their boss.
>
> —Drake, *Performance Appraisals*, p. 6

Employees have been known to storm out of offices, resign positions, and resort to violence based on "bad" evaluations. Generally appraisals, generate unpleasant emotions. Tears flow even after positive evaluations that include any small "areas for improvement." Such reactions are built into the process and are generally reflective of past negative experiences. It is intuitive for most managers that the environment and circumstances created by performance appraisals is just faulty, and it nurtures negativity.

Employees have been known to storm out of offices, resign positions, and resort to violence based on "bad" evaluations.

Solution: Abandon the use of traditional performance appraisals.

If employees and supervisors dislike appraisals, what is the benefit in continuing to use them? Supervisors are not good at serving as judges and subordinates are not simply passive objects to be rated. Employees dislike appraisal but want, need, and appreciate feedback. The only solution is to abandon the use of appraisals and utilize systems of performance management that do not include ratings and appraisal, but instead emphasize feedback, information exchange, and mutual support.

Employees dislike appraisal but want, need, and appreciate feedback.

Performance Conversations® Building Blocks

The Performance Conversations® model does not embrace the unnatural and disagreeable practice of passing judgment on another individual called an appraisal. The Performance Conversations® approach avoids appraisal in favor of a system of structured feedback. Employees like feedback and they get numerous structured opportunities to give and receive it during the *Progress Reviews* found in the model.

Summary of Human Fallacies

Supervisors are human and cannot overcome the shortcomings of appraisal system design. Furthermore the natural reaction of supervisors and subordinates to the idea of evaluation blocks their ability to give and receive open, honest, and clear feedback. Employees must be involved in the performance management process to provide information that fully characterizes performance because their supervisors cannot view all aspects of their performance all of the time. Supervisors must first receive full and complete training on supervision before they can expect to implement an effective performance management process.

Fallacies, Truths, and Solutions—A Listing of Human Fallacies

Fallacy I: Supervisors are omniscient; they see and know all.

Truth: Supervisors do not see everything, miss some things, and often take vacations

Solution: Train supervisors very well in the science of supervision and require employees to be highly involved in the performance management process.

Fallacy J: A well-trained supervisor can overcome rater bias.

Truth: Most of us are human.

Solution: Either hire androids, or abandon the use of rating systems and require employees to be involved in the tracking of their efforts.

Fallacy K: Supervisors and employees see value in performance appraisals.

Truth: Rarely are kind words spoken about the performance appraisal process.

Solution: Abandon the use of traditional performance appraisals.

Quick Reference Points

Chapter 6

- To err is human.

- Appraisal systems that use only the supervisors' observations are incomplete.

- Supervisors take vacations, and they miss some things.

- Employees must be involved in their own performance management.

- Managers must be trained to supervise before they can manager effectively.

- Managers must be trained on the performance management process before they employ it.

- Rater bias (human foibles) is inevitable and therefore compromises all appraisal systems.

- Managers hate appraisals.

- Employees hate appraisals even more.

- Managers cannot be coaches and judges at the same time.

- Appraisals are counterproductive.

CHAPTER 7

Fallacies of Instrument Design

WHERE PERFORMANCE APPRAISAL THEORY meets practice is with instrument design. We have refuted the assumptions and premises upon which performance appraisals are based. In this section we dissect and dismantle the devices employed to actually measure and rate performance. In short, performance appraisals are doomed for failure before they are implemented because their foundation is weak and their methods are ineffective. Not much success can come from a questionable idea with incomplete tools; nonetheless some organizations still use them.

Fallacy L: Appraisal instruments contain all the important dimensions of performance.

Fallacy M: Appraising only performance factors is enough.

Fallacy N: Progressive discipline occurs inside of the performance appraisal process.

Fallacy O: Performance appraisal is a reliable basis for making administrative decisions.

Scenario L – But, What About This?

Manager: *Jasmine, your evaluation this year will be a 4.5 out of 5.*
Employee: *I don't remember any event that should have lowered my score from a 5—I usually always get 5's. Why did I get a 4.5?*
Manager: *4.5 is respectable.*
Employee: *Perhaps for you 4.5 is an okay score, but for me all 5's is my goal. Can you tell me specifically why I did not rate a 5?*

Manager: *You did a good job on most things. You did great on workflow prepara-tion, workflow gap analysis and preparing the documentation. However, you did not do as well on the actual implementation of the software.*

Employee: *But what about the training, job aids, and training manuals? You said I did well on those also.*

Manager: *Yes, you performed well on all of those, but they aren't as important as the actual implementation. If training is fabulously delivered but the system does not perform well because it was not implemented well, it is for naught.*

Employee: *That's not fair.*

Performance Conversations

Manager: *Jasmine, you did a good job on most things. You did great on the manu-als and the actual training seminar, but you did not do as well on the system imple-mentation.*

Employee: *Yes, I was working on the project files, the multimedia software, and the new support materials as you can see from the entries in my Performance Log.*

Manager: *I did not know you were spending so much time on files or the new sup-port materials. That's good, but our emphasis over the past several months should have been on the entire implementation. There are a lot of loose ends there that need our attention.*

Employee: *I'm glad that you mention that now, otherwise I could spend a lot of time working on project files and the multimedia software since they are areas that really need some attention.*

Manager: *It is good that we talked about those during this Progress Review. As you know, things change from time to time and we need to shift emphasis where our attention is needed most.*

Employee: *That makes sense. It sounds like you would prefer that we make sure that each project is implemented and successful 100 percent before moving on to the next thing, right?*

Performance Conversations® focus on what is important now—priorities, goals, successes, problems, or things that may have changed. With traditional appraisal there is a false assumption that the only things that we can and should pay attention to are those things measured on a static evaluation instrument. Performance is too dynamic to be reduced down to a form. Managing perfor-mance is a process that is regulated in periodic Progress Reviews in the Perfor-mance Conversations® approach.

Fallacy L

[A] performance appraisal instrument might list only a few of the employee's tasks. Tasks that an employee excels in might be forgotten or ignored and tasks that an employee bungles might be emphasized. For example, interpersonal relations can be a very important aspect of performance. Yet, if it is not part of the performance appraisal form, its absence can result in deficient appraisals.

—Johnson and Kaupins, "Keeping Lies Out of the Performance Appraisal," p. 3

Fallacy L: Appraisal instruments contain all the important dimensions of performance.

Truth: It is not possible to account for all performance dimensions for all positions and for all types of employees on any single appraisal instrument.

No single form can describe and capture all the performance information necessary for a complete Performance Review.

How Many Performance Dimensions Are There?

For any given job there are probably dozens of different performance dimensions. Here are some typical measures of performance:

• Job knowledge	• Creativity
• Quality of work	• Problem-solving
• Quantity of work	• Decision-making
• Adaptability	• Fiscal management
• Dependability	• Personnel management
• Interpersonal relations	• Staff development
• Communication skills	• Planning and assessment
• Attitude	• Professional development
• Attendance	• Employee diversification
• Initiative	• Technological competence
• Knowledge of the company	• Time management
• Professionalism	• Professionalism
• Time management	• Computer literacy
• Efficiency	

Performance dimensions can be a combination of traits, behaviors, and results used to measure or describe desired performance. There are dimensions specific to the individual, specific to the goals of the organization, or that are only related to certain kinds of positions, such as managerial responsibilities. The number and type of performance criteria are limitless. No single form can describe and capture all the performance information necessary for a complete Performance Review.

Job Specific Performance Dimensions

Experts wisely advise that good job performance dimensions are based upon the essential functions of each job as noted in the job description. However, the challenge then becomes how to compare individuals across jobs, departments, and throughout the organization. A person with more difficult tasks might have a more difficult chance of succeeding than a person with fewer responsibilities and easier tasks, if they are evaluated on the same standard rating scale. This is yet another example of where performance appraisal theory and practice are disconnected.

We Can't Easily Measure Qualitative Things

> Managers tend to measure what is *easiest* to measure, thereby bypassing qualitative aspects of a job, such as customer service or interpersonal relations, in favor of quantitative ones, such as volume or accuracy.
> —Robinson, *How to Conduct Employee Performance Appraisals*, p. A-2

The subjectivity involved in measuring qualitative factors is a breeding ground for disagreement and conflict. The supervisor's judgment of the presence and richness of performance can be subject to interpretation. Such judgments are most problematic when they are given as ratings or labels. Since rating qualitative factors is so difficult, organizations generally rate only those factors that appear to be totally objective. Thus, measurements are not necessarily taken of all factors important to performance, but only those factors that can be measured.

Only That Which Is on the Form Is Important

The performance indicators that are tracked on the appraisal instrument are elevated in importance as compared to those indicators that are not included on the form. The performance appraisal instrument can unintentionally send mixed signals about what is deemed important. These mixed signals imply that things "not counted, do not count." Selected employees will only do those

things that are evaluated and will avoid tasks that are not appraised or rewarded.

These mixed signals imply that things "not counted, do not count."

Behavior Dimensions Are Equally Important

There are numerous examples of outstanding performance that is marred by
inexcusable behavior. Most often performance appraisal instruments contain
many indices to measure performance, but do not include reliable methods of
measuring behavior. These instruments, by design, are incapable of fully managing performance.

Individual, Departmental, or Organizational Dimensions

The strategic purpose of performance management instruments is met by ensuring that work performed by individuals is aligned with the needs of the organization. Individual employees should fully understand how their work tasks
advance the organization's goals. Most instruments focus on the individual and
assume that if the individual does well, the organization does well. But the individual can also do substantial work that does not generate revenue, work that
inhibits overall team output, or work that creates an environment that causes
hatred and discontentment among coworkers. Individual and organizational
performance dimensions should be explicitly linked and coordinated.

Performance Requirements Change

Will performance dimensions defined by HR and consultants on a company-
wide instrument in 2004 be current in 2008? Should the performance appraisal
instrument change each year, or as the company's needs change? Is it possible to
design an instrument that is change-proof? If we change every few years, will we
ever get enough training to become proficient on any one instrument?

One Size Does Not Fit All

"If the only tool you have is a hammer, then every problem looks like a nail,"
the old saying goes. The work tasks of a custodian are substantially different
from those of a vice president. Not only are their tasks different, but the overall
context of their positions is different. It would seem obvious that mental health
counselors and accountants would have different performance dimensions, as
would production line workers and sales managers. It would be a wasted effort
to evaluate executives on their attendance as they almost certainly work almost
every day of the week whether they are physically at work, at home, on vaca-

tion, or traveling. Likewise, a performance dimension that measures strategic planning should be omitted in the appraisal of non-exempt employees and many middle managers. It is imperative that organizations understand that the use of one standard performance management instrument to attempt to appraise all performance across departments, functions, levels, and professions is ill-advised.

Multiple Goals and Multiple Conflicts

> PA systems fail largely because they are designed with conflicting goals.
> —Drake, *Performance Appraisals*, p. 11

One of the failings of many performance management systems is they attempt to measure too many factors on a single form. Experts say the performance management systems generally have three different goals: strategic, developmental, and administrative. They are used strategically to align individual efforts with organizational goals. Administrative uses include making personnel decisions about pay, promotions, training opportunities, and layoffs. The developmental purpose is met when the process helps to direct individual training and professional development. Expecting the performance management process to accomplish all of these broad and disparate goals is wishful thinking. Additionally, the three goals are compounded with many other uses. Here are a few of the numerous applications of performance management systems:

- Performance measurement and rating (appraisal)

- Pay administration (merit and incentive pay)

- Core competencies or organization-wide performance standards

- Individual development plans

- Discipline

- Goal setting

- Review employees of all experience levels—rookies, mid-career employees, veterans

- Review employees of all organizational levels (non-exempt, exempt, professional, management, executive)

- Review all professions (custodians, salespeople, accountants, computer programmers)

- Self-evaluation

- Quantitative performance criteria

- Qualitative performance criteria

- Management-specific performance criteria

- Departmental/division-specific performance criteria

- Strategic alignment

- Behavior management

Conflict between the goals, purposes, and uses of appraisal tools is inevitable. Too many attempted purposes will dilute the effectiveness of any process away from the primary purpose—performance improvement.

Too many attempted purposes will dilute the effectiveness of any process away from the primary purpose—performance improvement.

Length of Instrument Inversely Related to Completion Percentage

When organizations attempt to do too much with their performance management system, the form used becomes too lengthy. The longer and more involved an instrument, the greater the likelihood the instrument will not be completed at all. There is also a lower probability that it will be completed thoroughly and accurately. A four-page appraisal instrument requires a greater commitment of time and effort than a two-page instrument. There have also been stories of six-, eight-, or even nine-paged instruments. Such lengthy instruments are created because they attempt to achieve multiple and contradictory purposes.

Solution: Performance management systems should consist of a *process*, instead of a form, with a narrowly defined purpose—performance improvement.

The more organizations try to do with the performance management instruments, the greater the likelihood the system will fail. They try to build a system to fix several problems, only to end up with one that fixes none. Performance management systems are often used as a poor surrogate for effective day-to-day supervision and other management actions. Organizations try to cram a year's worth of supervisory activities into a one-hour review and a two-page document.

Performance management systems should be a *process*, not a document. The essential ingredient of the process should be good supervision with frequent and specific feedback. The goal of the process should be singular—performance improvement (replicate good performance, correct bad performance, and generally improve upon all performance). The Performance Conversations® model facilitates continuous productivity improvements.

Performance Conversations® Building Blocks

The essence of the Performance Conversations® approach is that it is a series of discussions over time. The ongoing nature of the **Progress Reviews,** the continuous data collection in **Performance Logs** and the **Performance Portfolio,** the focus on the future, and continuous improvement defines a systematic management process. There is no magical form; Performance Conversations® manages, adjusts and regulates performance through the use of ongoing dialogue.

Scenario M – One Bad Apple or Bittersweet Superstar

Performance Confrontation (Traditional Appraisal)

Manager: *Johnny, I'm reluctant to give you the highest rating, but . . .*

Employee: *I bring in the numbers, Boss, you know I do!*

Manager: *Yes, you do, but you continue to have little situations with your coworkers.*

Employee: *Please. They are just jealous and are trying to make me look bad. If they were to work harder, they would not have time to complain about me.*

Manager: *That might be true, but you have given them something to complain about. You have been accused of talking down to others, being rude, and making remarks about how well you are doing. You are not much of a team player.*

Employee: *I'm here to be a superstar, not a member of some team. I will not compromise my great performance for some worthless team effort. It should be every man for himself; work hard and just bring in the numbers.*

Manager: *Well, I'm going to go ahead and give you the highest rating because team work and attitude are not dimensions on the evaluation form. I gave you highest marks for exceeding sales goals; growing revenue for new and existing product lines; maintaining appropriate cost of sales ratios; and exceeding cross selling goals for our other divisions. But I must say that I'm not happy with your inability to be a team player.*

Employee: *Thanks, Boss. I was really working hard to get that raise and with these ratings, I think it is a slam dunk—good thing for me that an annoying team rating is not on the form, huh?*

Performance Conversations®

Manager: *Johnny, let's have a conversation about your total performance.*

Employee: *I bring in the numbers, Boss. You know I do!*

Manager: *Yes, you do, but you continue to have little situations with your coworkers.*

Employee: *Please. They are just jealous and are trying to make me look bad. If they were to work harder, they would not have time to complain about me.*

Manager: *That might be true, but you have given them something to complain about. You have been accused of talking down to others, being rude, and making remarks about how well you are doing. You are not much of a team player.*

Employee: *I guess the truth hurts some of them.*

Manager: *Everything you do affects how the department does and everything you do reflects on yourself and the department. So, your team work and attitude are just as important as your productivity.*

Employee: *So, you are saying it does not matter that I put up better numbers than everyone else.*

Manager: *That's not what I'm saying. What I'm saying is that your performance certainly is based on outcomes, and you do a great job in that area—you are the best. But your teamwork is not as good as your productivity. In order to be a consummate player, you must also excel at your ability to work with others.*

Employee: *So, you are saying I don't have to try as hard, I can just be nicer to people and you will be happy.*

Manager: *No, what I'm saying is that you excel in most areas and you can excel in all areas if you are willing to focus your energies there as well. As a matter of fact, since you are so good at producing the numbers, you should consider sharing your excellent techniques with coworkers. By training them, I'm sure that they will all get better.*

Employee: *I'm sure that I can teach them a thing or two.*

Manager: *I can hear the sarcasm in your voice. But, you are right. You can teach them a thing or two, and that's exactly what I'm asking you to do.*

Using the Performance Conversations® approach, everything that affects performance is accounted for in discussions about work—all efforts, outcomes, and behaviors. Many traditional appraisals are narrowly designed and focus on outcomes only. They miss the opportunity to manage the other performance indicators such as attitude and efforts which also affect the work and work environment.

Fallacy M

Performance deals with knowledge, skills, and abilities needed to meet job-task expectations. Conformance deals with adherence to rules and procedures mandated by law, safety requirements, and management expectations. Performance appraisal systems should not accommodate the contrasting and often conflicting requirements found in the different constructs of performance and conformance.

—Benham, "Performance Appraisal: A Radical View," p. 155

Fallacy M: Appraising only performance factors is enough.

Truth: Bad behavior undermines good performance.

The late Professor Philip Benham must be acknowledged for his contributions to exposing Fallacy M. His progressive thinking on the subject benefits us all. In an article entitled "Performance Appraisal: A Radical View," (Benham 2001) he advocated distinguishing between the constructs of conformance and performance. He generously offered his thoughts and advice to me after reviewing an early draft of this book.

Behavior and Performance

Behavior and performance are two sides of the same coin and are inseparable. Both must be present for performance to be credible. The preferable approach would be to have two separate systems to address them, as the goals of performance management and behavior management are different. As Professor Benham advises, the requirements of the two systems conflict:

A real, but often overlooked, part of the problem is the role conflict the process causes many managers. The dilemma for many managers is how to combine criticism and punishment with praise and reward in a manner that motivates commitment to improved performance.

—Benham, "Performance Appraisal: A Radical View," p. 156

Rule violations that are blatant, willful, and inconsistent with organizational decorum and effectiveness are destructive and should not be tolerated. Punishment can be appropriate response to such actions.

All behavior at work will, on some level, impact performance or characterizes an individual's contributions to their employer.

Behavior, Conformance, and Performance

The range of human behavior is almost limitless, and it is impossible to publish a policy or rule that would define all unacceptable behavior possible. Nonetheless, bad behavior in any form compromises good performance. Supervisors can address bad behavior with two separate tools, the performance management process and the progressive discipline process. Behavior problems that directly involve and impact performance are governed by performance management; behavior that indirectly involves performance or organizational citizenship can be addressed in the progressive discipline process. While it would be ideal for behavior problems to fall neatly within one category, the reality is that one or both of these tools will likely be utilized in many behavior challenges. All behavior at work will, on some level, impact performance or characterizes an individual's contributions to their employer.

Behavior that affects performance comes in three different varieties. First, aberrant behaviors are those things that are simply foolish, work related or not. Second, nonconformance or rule violations are another form of unacceptable behavior. Behaviors such as a lack of attention to detail or follow-through can also create bad performance; these examples of not following proper procedures illustrate the third kind of behavior that negatively affects productivity.

Aberrant Behavior

Bad behavior cannot be anticipated but still undermines good performance by creating an unproductive, negative work environment. Examples are individuals misusing company property, engaging in trysts at work, using illegal substances, and sleeping on the job. There are times that even with these "clear examples of bad behavior" terminations are overturned because there was no "specific rule" that governed the particular behavior. Organizations would be prudent to create a rule or policy that says, "Any behavior deemed to be inconsistent with the mission and goals of the organization, or perceived to be in conflict with organizational interests, shall be subject to disciplinary procedures." Organizations should not endorse or tolerate unacceptable behavior. These matters should be subject to the progressive discipline process, to include immediate dismissal at the acute violation threshold of the progressive discipline doctrine.

Nonconformance not only undermines performance; ultimately, it undermines the entire organization.

Following Rules

Following rules, laws, or policies, or what Professor Benham calls *conformance*, are necessary for all organizations to preserve order and efficiency. Conformance is necessary for people to work together in any group or organization. As advised by Professor Benham, nonconformance behaviors should be dealt with swiftly and effectively through disciplinary procedures. This allows employees to refocus their attention back to the work at hand as soon as possible.

> In maintaining conformance standards, managers must define their role as counselor and enforcer. Counselors are not coaches. Counselors confront miscreant behavior promptly and make it clear that the offending behavior will not be tolerated. They are firm and unambiguous in tone, but not demeaning. They also offer help when personal problems appear to be at the root of nonconforming behavior.
> —Benham, "Performance Appraisal: A Radical View," p. 162

Enforcing compliance should be swift, stern, and not necessarily progressive. Nonconformance not only undermines performance; ultimately, it undermines the entire organization.

Following Instructions

Failing to follow instructions or procedures is usually a performance issue that can be managed within the performance management process. In most circumstances, it is likely to be a training or comprehension challenge. Standard supervision, good management, or training and development will normally resolve such situations. Such circumstances are a shortfall in knowledge, skills, or abilities, not behavioral problems.

Good Performance Is What I Say It Is

There is clearly more than one way to play the game. Therefore, coaches are allowed the discretion to determine what style of play their teams will employ. Likewise, managers define *good* within their domain. Yet, the belief in most performance management systems is that performance is an objective idea.

The truth is that good performance is how the manager defines it. Ideally, this definition of performance will be based upon factual information, agreed upon standards, clearly identified expectations, company policies and procedures, and appropriate input from the employee. If the employee and the manager do not agree on the definition of good performance (after working hard and trying to negotiate a standard by which all agree), the tie goes to the manager.

The manager is ultimately responsible to superiors for the quality performance of subordinates. Therefore, if good performance by all other measures is not considered good by the manager, staff members should be required to work, act, and perform in a manner consistent with what the supervisor reasons is best. This is the discretion and responsibility that most organizations give to managers. There are two caveats that should be noted with this perspective. If the manager's standards are biased, unfair, unethical, or illegal, the manager's actions should not be defended, supported, or tolerated by the organization. Second, the manager's standards should be reviewed periodically by superiors to determine if they are consistent with organizational policies, and practices.

Solution: Behavior, conformance, and performance should all be managed within the performance management process.

> Performance and conformance are separate constructs. They require separate, albeit frequently complementary, administrative systems.
> —Benham, "Performance Appraisal: A Radical View," p. 164

Behavior and performance are two independent, but interdependent, performance dimensions. They must be managed together and separately as the individual circumstance requires. Organizations should properly diagnose behavior issues as either aberrant behavior or work-specific noncompliance. Work related behavior that is willful or neglectful is nonconformance and should not be confused with poor performance caused by a gap in knowledge, skills or abilities. Supervisors must use the appropriate tool for the appropriate challenge, performance management or progressive discipline. Nonetheless, the end goal is the same—good performance.

Performance Conversations® Building Blocks

The Performance Conversations® model incorporates the solution to Fallacy M in that it tracks efforts, outcomes, and behaviors. Anything that an employee or manager does or fails to do is an indicator of performance. All indicators of performance are tracked by entries into *Performance Logs*. Traditional appraisals restrict their purview to seven to ten indices on an appraisal instrument, when in reality the number and type of indicators of performance are limitless.

Scenario N – Now I Know!

Performance Confrontations (Traditional Appraisal)

Manager: *Terry, I've some concerns with how you have been handling our Canadian clients.*

Employee: *Concerns?*

Manager: *It has just come to my attention that you have not been providing them with all of the support that they have requested.*

Employee: *I know we had one issue last fall, but I got them the information they needed in time for their new project.*

Manager: *That's true according to their Chief Operations Officer. However, we need to talk about how you have handled their account overall. As you know they are one of our biggest customers and your work there does not speak well of your performance.*

Employee: *But you just gave me an "Outstanding" rating on my performance evaluation. I thought I was handling all of my work well.*

Manager: *The matter I want to discuss with you is not on your evaluation form, and this information just came to my attention.*

Employee: *Then why did you say that I was doing outstanding if you have a problem with my performance?*

Manager: *They are two separate matters.*

Employee: *This is confusing to me. Am I doing a good job or not?*

Performance Conversations®

Manager: *Terry, I've some concerns with how you have been handling our Canadian clients.*

Employee: *Concerns?*

Manager: *It has just come to my attention that you have not been providing them with all of the support that they have requested.*

Employee: *I know we had one issue last fall, but I got them the information they needed in time for their new project.*

Manager: *I did not know there was an issue last fall. We met several times last fall in our **Progress Reviews** and I'm disappointed that you did not mention any problems.*

Employee: *I did not mention it because it was a small matter that I quickly addressed and the problem went away.*

Manager: *The problem did not go away. You have not followed your part of our agreement and our way of doing business. Every time we meet at our regular Progress Reviews, I ask you about the status of each of your projects and if there have been any snafus with them. You obviously did not fully disclose what was going on in Toronto.*

Employee: *I did not want to alarm you or make a big deal out of it.*

Manager: *My role is to support you and help you overcome challenges. If you had informed me earlier, I could have intervened and we could have prevented the issue from getting bigger. Now the problem has reached our corporate office. Since this is a major infraction, we will have to document the matter and create a plan of action for preventing similar issues from happening again.*

Discipline occurs when performance management efforts have failed. It should occur separately from the normal supervisory process. Performance Conversations®, through the use of periodic Progress Reviews, detect and address problems when they are corrections and before adjustments are made due to discipline.

Fallacy N

Use performance management to note success and improvement in meeting job results and in demonstrating job-related behaviors required to obtain results. Use progressive discipline to note failure in complying with rules and procedures established by law and by management (Benham, 2001, p. 160).

> **Fallacy N:** Progressive discipline occurs inside of the performance appraisal process.

> **Truth:** Discipline should not occur within the performance management process.

The Discipline Problem Is Not Listed on the Performance Appraisal Instrument

There are numerous reasons why employees might be disciplined, but very few of these reasons appear on the actual performance appraisal instrument. The actual instrument may be designed with seven or eight performance dimensions, as well as sections for professional development, standards, goal setting, but rarely behavioral factors. A memorandum that describes the performance problem and appropriate discipline is usually best for the situation.

Performance appraisal instruments are too general and are not designed to deal with discipline. Appraisals may be attachments and can be evidence, but they should not be used to record discipline events. In practical terms, there is not even any space on such instruments to write such information. A model approach to progressive discipline includes four elements that should be included in any letter of reprimand. They are (1) a description of the specific performance or behavior involved; (2) how this bad situation affects others or the organization; (3) what specific actions the employee must take to correct the situation; and (4) the time frame for a follow-up, progress check, or remediation.

Behavior anomalies are seldom listed on appraisal instruments, because human behavior is not predicable. It would be difficult for a succinct performance tool to address such issues as that of an exceptional employee who withholds information from a coworker because the coworker will not pay him for a bet the two had on a football game—a real event! Only progressive discipline can address such matters.

Performance appraisal instruments are too general and are not designed to deal with discipline.

Timing of the Problem and Scheduled Evaluations

Performance appraisals are summaries, and discipline needs to focus on specific issues. Many performance issues may materialize, be addressed, be corrected, and then disappear between scheduled Performance Reviews. Furthermore, it would be foolish to conduct a full performance appraisal interview out of cycle to address one specific issue that may or may not be a factor on the actual instrument.

Many performance issues may materialize, be addressed, be corrected, and then disappear between scheduled Performance Reviews.

Progressive Discipline and Appraisal—Perfect Alignment Is Not Possible

The normal four-step process for discipline is (1) counseling, (2) verbal reprimands, (3) written reprimands, and (4) suspension. The steps are not aligned with the normal performance appraisal processes. Additionally, performance appraisals cannot address acute disciplinary issues, which are specific infractions that are so severe that immediate termination could result. The documentation of an acute termination event on an appraisal instrument would be unnecessary. The termination letter that states the reason for the dismissal is all that would be required. Indeed, in most cases, the presence of progressive discipline is evidence of performance management failure.

Performance Improvement Plan

Good disciplinary letters outline the steps an employee must take to correct the performance or behavior problem. They are specific to an issue. They describe what quality and quantity of future performance, or corrective behavior is necessary to prevent additional disciplinary action. Also, due to the dynamic nature of human behavior, some issues are confounded with personal problems, so a referral to an employee assistance program (EAP) may also be included in the remedial action. The discipline letter also states the time frame and includes a warning that noncompliance will result in further discipline. The plan of action is tailored to prevent past shortcomings from reoccurring and focuses attention forward. Disciplinary issues are ill suited to a performance appraisal instrument.

The Rest of the Story

Performance appraisals do not tell the full story or provide the necessary context, details, and history of a performance problem. Appraisals are too focused on summarizing and rating performance to deal with particular performance problems. If minor errors over a long period of time require disciplinary action, appraisals are unlikely to provide enough information to describe the problem adequately. Consistent poor performance over time should be addressed as soon as it is noticed, and certainly not delayed until a performance appraisal event is scheduled.

Discipline without Punishment

In the book *Discipline without Punishment*, author Dick Grote advocates focusing on correcting the problem, not punishing the offender. This is consistent with the twenty-first-century management idea of providing feedback, not appraisal. The recommendation is not to point fingers or catch someone doing something wrong; the goal is to reproduce good performance and therefore performance rehabilitation. The desired outcome of discipline is to prevent the problem from happening again, not punishment.

Solution: Progressive discipline and discipline without punishment should occur separately from the performance management process.

When an individual is being disciplined, the supervisor wants the employee to acknowledge the issue, to understand fully the deeds that caused the disciplinary action, and to understand exactly what must be done to prevent a reoccurrence. Progressive discipline is quite dissimilar from performance appraisals that were designed to measure and rate performance. The progressive discipline process should be used when performance management efforts have failed or when the employee engages in willful nonconformance behaviors. The goals of performance management and progressive discipline are incompatible and should not occur in a single interaction with an employee. The purpose, goals, and methodology of the two systems are different, and although complementary, both should have separate and distinct management systems.

Performance Conversations® Building Blocks

Just as the solution to Fallacy N advises, the Performance Conversations® model keeps discipline and punishment separate. The Performance Conversations® model has a single purpose—performance improvement. Nonetheless, the Performance Conversations® approach does complement the progressive discipline process. All of the data necessary to justify discipline or a termination is routinely collected and recorded on the **Performance Log** and in the **Performance Portfolio** as they contain all the good, bad, and neutral indicators of performance.

Scenario O – Based Upon What?

Performance Confrontations (Traditional Appraisal)

Manager: *Gloria, you will get a 3 percent raise this year.*
Employee: *Only 3 percent? I was expecting to get 6 percent because I got a good appraisal earlier this year.*
Manager: *Yes, your evaluation went well. But as you know, our raises are only partially based upon the evaluation.*
Employee: *If the evaluation didn't matter, why did we do it? What else could I've done to earn more?*
Manager: *I'm not sure, but raises are based upon performance, seniority, division success, and the need for the company to retain certain key skills in certain departments.*
Employee: *Will my raise be the highest in the department?*
Manager: *Why do you ask?*
Employee: *You gave me the highest rating, didn't you?*
Manager: *Yes, I did. But several people also got an "Ouststanding" mark.*
Employee: *I think I do better than most people in the department, and everyone gets the same mark? Obviously these appraisals don't mean much.*

Performance Conversations®

Manager: *Gloria, I'm pleased to tell you that you will get a 4 percent raise effective immediately.*

Employee: *Great. Thank you, I did not know that an increase was coming.*

Manager: *It is in recognition of your contributions to the department and company. I and others have noticed how well you are doing. Every **Progress Review** we have had adds more credence to your professional reputation. Thank you for your good work.*

Employee: *I appreciate you noticing that I've made a lot of changes in how I work, and those changes are making a difference.*

Manager: *As you know, Hamilton Enterprises does not tie increases to appraisals or anything like that, but your performance continues to be stellar. Thus, I recommended to senior management that we recognize your exceptional contributions. The evidence in your **Performance Portfolio** was compelling. The examples of your work convinced everyone that you were worthy of this recognition.*

Employee: *Thank you again. It is nice to work at a place where you are appreciated.*

The Performance Conversations® approach recognizes that performance is managed by a number of organizational elements and that performance information comes from a variety of sources. Therefore, decisions about performance, organizational rewards, and other personnel actions are made in context with other information. Traditional appraisals are ineffective and flawed. Decisions that are made based upon them are not sound.

Fallacy O

Fallacy O: Performance appraisal is a reliable basis for making administrative decisions.

Truth: There at least fifteen flaws attributed to performance appraisals, and any or all of them undermine the administrative decisions based upon their use (see above).

For dozens of reasons, traditional performance appraisal systems are not valid or reliable, and therefore are not a good basis upon which to make administrative decisions such as pay raises, promotions, training opportunities, or layoffs. The sheer number of potential pitfalls of appraisal should be cause for concern. Even if only one or two drawbacks apply to any given situation, it is sufficient to acknowledge that decisions based upon performance appraisals are unsound. The performance appraisals process is fundamentally flawed, and decisions made largely from the information generated by them are equally fallible.

Even if only one or two drawbacks apply to any given situation, it is sufficient to acknowledge that decisions based upon performance appraisals are unsound.

As indicated earlier in Fallacy J, information generated in the performance appraisal process is only one of the many factors that should be used to make administrative decisions. To suggest that it is the only factor by which an individual is given a merit increase or upon which administrative decisions are made is simply not true. Some examples of other elements included in making administrative decisions are the comparative performance of others, the economic condition of the company, company need, employee seniority, and employee behavior.

Furthermore, ratings are not reliable. Traditional performance appraisal systems are flawed in their design, implementation, and use. Supervisors seldom are effective in using such systems because the assumptions that guide how we use performance appraisals are unsubstantiated. Using performance appraisals as the centerpiece by which organizational decisions are made is simply nonsensical.

Solution: Abandon the use of traditional performance appraisals.

Traditional appraisal systems that rely upon ratings should be abandoned, and performance management systems that are designed to generate a reasonable amount of quantitative and qualitative information should be used instead. Smarter performance management systems will emphasize feedback and information exchange. This information should be integrated with other organizational information to make good organizational decisions. It is high time to discuss alternatives to traditional appraisals that actually improve individual performance and employee relationships.

Performance Conversations® Building Blocks

The Performance Conversations® model is superior to traditional appraisals because it gathers a large amount of evidence of performance through its **Performance Log** and **Performance Portfolio**. This evidence is better than the brief summary of performance often found on traditional appraisal instruments. The model also acknowledges that performance management systems and their byproducts are only one of several organizational systems that provide information for organizational decision making.

Summary of Instrument Design

Organizations attempt to have their performance appraisal system do so many disparate things that they often work against one another. These processes become so complex that few are able to use them correctly, or understand the hidden motives behind these long and involved instruments. Additionally, performance appraisal instruments are limited in what they track and measure. They cannot account for all the dimensions of performance. Nor can such tools properly manage different levels of employees, in different jobs or professions.

Typical instruments omit behavior criteria and other equally important qualitative factors of performance. They also do not distinguish between rule violations and performance challenges, each of which requires a different intervention. Discipline is appropriate for rule violations or willful neglect. Coaching and supervision are appropriate responses to gaps in knowledge, skills, and abilities.

When organizations try to manage performance, rate performance, set goals, support individual development, publicize core competencies, and discipline malfeasants all within a single process and on a single form, it is not surprising that traditional performance appraisal systems are guaranteed to fail. Better supervision and a more enlightened approach to managing performance are necessary to lead people in the twenty-first century. Enter the Performance Conversations® Model.

Fallacies, Truths, and Solutions—Fallacies of Instrument Design

Fallacy L: Appraisal instruments contain all the important dimensions of performance.

Truth: It is not possible to account for all performance dimensions for all positions, and for all types of employees on any single appraisal instrument.

Solution: Performance management systems should consist of a *process*, instead of a form, with a narrowly defined purpose—performance improvement.

Fallacy M: Appraising only performance factors is enough.

Truth: Bad behavior undermines good performance.

Solution: Behavior, conformance, and performance should all be managed within the performance management process.

Fallacy N: Progressive discipline occurs inside of the performance appraisal process.

Truth: Discipline should not occur within the performance management process.

Solution: Progressive discipline and discipline without punishment should occur separately from the performance management process.

Fallacy O: Performance appraisal is a reliable basis for making administrative decisions.

Truth: There at least fifteen flaws attributed to performance appraisals; any or all of them undermine the administrative decisions based upon their use.

Solution: Abandon the use of traditional performance appraisals.

Quick Reference Points

Chapter 7

- There are hundreds of different performance dimensions that can be tracked.

- Appraisal instruments contain only seven to ten dimensions, on average.

- Appraisal systems do not usually account for qualitative dimensions, or behavior.

- Organizations try to do too much with their performance management system, such as appraisal, strategic alignment, pay administration, and career development.

- Too many goals for appraisal systems cause conflicts and long, cumbersome instruments.

- Good behavior can enhance performance; bad behavior can overshadow performance.

- Performance management systems must also manage behavior.

- The goal of performance management is to improve all performance; the goal of progressive discipline is to address specific problems.

- There should be a separate system to administer discipline.

- For all the reasons we have spent four chapters discussing, appraisals do not work. Therefore, making administrative decisions based upon them is really not a good idea.

PART III

The Solutions

The effectiveness of an appraisal [performance management] system is determined by the quality of the communication between the manager and staff member, not by multiple raters, complex scoring methods, or the form used.

—J. D. Drake

CHAPTER 8

A Review of Potential Solutions

The net effect of fifty years of intense efforts at improving the process has failed to yield any form of appraisal that can consistently and accurately measure an individual's performance over an extended period of time. This may be somewhat overstated in the case of very simple, highly structured, repetitive jobs, but it certainly holds true for more complex jobs, including managerial and professional jobs that are most routinely subject to appraisal.

—T. Coens and M. Jenkins

PERFORMANCE APPRAISALS DO NOT work. Here are a few solutions that have been discussed to help organizations overcome the fallacies of appraisal:

Solution A: Design, adjust, and manage the organization as an interdependent system that supports performance. Integrate HR systems to include performance management and align all performance management initiatives with the organizational culture and environment.

Solution B: The performance management process should be future oriented and focused on information, feedback, and description, rather than measurement, evaluation, and documentation.

Solution C: Hold supervisors accountable for their staff development, supervision, results, and participation in the performance management process (completed, on time, and accurate).

Solution D: Formal, informal, ongoing, periodic, micro-level, and macro-level feedback should all be used to manage performance.

Solution E: Providing challenging, meaningful work; creating a nurturing and supportive environment; and involving employees in decisions that affect their work—these imperatives encourage pride in workmanship and personal growth. This is the key to sustained motivation.

Solution F: Abandon the use of ratings, and emphasize description, diagnosis, and discussion instead.

Solution G: Do not use traditional performance appraisals.

Solution H: Other management systems can be used to document performance and meet administrative requirements.

Solution I: Train managers and get employees involved in performance man-agement.

Solution J: Either hire androids, or abandon the use of rating systems and require employees to be involved in the tracking of their efforts.

Solution K: Abandon the use of traditional performance appraisals.

Solution L: Performance management systems should consist of a *process,* instead of a form, with a narrowly defined purpose—performance improvement.

Solution M: Behavior, conformance, and performance should all be managed within the performance management process.

Solution N: Progressive discipline and discipline without punishment should occur separately from the performance management process.

Solution O: Abandon the use of traditional performance appraisals.

The Performance Conversations® model incorporates all of the solutions to the Fallacies of Performance Appraisals. The model is also based on the imperative that traditional appraisals should be abandoned. A twenty-first century approach to management is needed to confront contemporary organizational challenges.

The four building blocks that redefine the performance management process in this new century are the collective solutions listed above, improved supervision; the right organizational context and support for the desired performance, and the Performance Conversations® model. In addition to these, the chapters that follow give managers and human resource professionals all of the tools needed to reinvent and drastically improve individual performance within their organizations.

Quick Reference Points

Chapter 8

- Don't use appraisals.

- Do something else—anything else.

- The Performance Conversations® model is a good choice.

CHAPTER 9

Prerequisites

Using performance appraisal systems without addressing the organizational culture complies only with appearances of fairness, not with a real proposition of change.

—H. D. Allender

BEFORE THE PERFORMANCE CONVERSATIONS® model can be fully employed, there are several prerequisites that must be in place, because no system for performance management can successfully manage performance alone. The four prerequisites are as follows:

1. Leaders must ensure that their organizational culture supports individual performance.

2. Work must be designed to keep employees engaged.

3. Supervisors must partner with employees in a way that allows them to do their best work.

4. Each human resource system within the organization must be aligned and coordinated to work with the performance management system to achieve optimal performance.

Each of these elements affect the character and quality of individual performance in and of themselves and they also support and reinforce the performance management system.

Culture First

Depending on whose perspective you choose to believe, as many as two-thirds to four-fifths of the causes of employee performance are attributable to the work environment, not the employees. If this is true,—in fact if it is only partially true—then one answer to the above question is, "Fix the systems in which our employees work!"

—Ripley, "Improving Employee Performance," p. 1

Simply defined, culture is "the way we do business around here." It is the personality of an organization, the expression of norms. Culture is the culmination of all the intentional and unintentional practices of an organization including its values, ethics, beliefs, assumptions, practices, policies, procedures, rituals, stories, heroes, villains, aspirations, and dysfunctions. It is the organization's social infrastructure. Culture is all of those intangible things that define an organization as unique.

Despite the fact that culture is difficult to define, or touch and feel, creating a productive culture is attainable. Since culture is so difficult to define in simple terms, case studies may best illustrate the meaning of culture and show how it directly impacts performance management. Four examples will demonstrate how culture drives performance within a variety of organizations through their policies, leadership, belief systems, practices, and programs:

- Southwest Airlines is often used as an example of an organization wherein employees have fun, but are also productive and efficient. When flying Southwest Airlines, it is immediately obvious that they are different. Instead of the blue sport coats worn by other airlines, a uniform of short pants and polo shirts is a summer standard for Southwest Airlines employees. The pilots and flight attendants might sing or tell jokes to passengers, but they are serious about customer service and efficient operations. The CEO and pilots have been known to pitch in to clean an aircraft in order to get it turned around for the next flight. In many organizational cultures, senior personnel would never "stoop so low" as to assist front line employees with their tasks. Their dress code implies a relaxed environment, their levity indicates a certain degree of openness, and the shared responsibilities of the front line and management solidify the importance of—above all—getting the job done. It is no surprise that they have been the most consistently profitable airline over the past decade.

- The 3M Corporation is known for having a culture of innovation that virtually invented the term and the practice of intraprenuership. This is the practice of letting internal employees freelance and create new products or services with the support (and often funding) of the organization. Employees can spend up to fifteen percent of their time working on side projects. If the project succeeds, the employee and their team are rewarded with recognition, pay, and promotions as appropriate. Obviously, this very successful organization also has a healthy tolerance for mistakes and failure.

- The United States Marine Corps is arguably the world's finest military organization. It has been foremost in battle for well over two centuries and its reputation has become synonymous with success. One may ask how and why an organization that draws its members from the same population as the U.S. Army, Navy, and Air Force can be so distinctively different. But the Marine Corps is unique in both its success and its culture. The culture is manifest in a variety of sayings and beliefs that all Marines share. One of its recruiting slogans tells part of the story, "The Few. The Proud. The Marines." Marine boot camp training at Parris Island is renowned for its difficulty, and the faint at heart are warned that earning the title Marine will not be easy, but the pride of wearing the title Marine is worth it. Their motto, *Semper Fidelis,* means *Always Faithful.* They say "Once a Marine, always a Marine"; there are no ex-Marines, only former Marines. This small elite group of men and women has created a fraternity that includes membership and a common camaraderie for life. The culture is also manifest in the practice that Marines do not leave their fallen comrades on the battlefield, but instead they risk life and limb to return Marines home for a proper burial. Despite the fact that their weapons, tactics, and resources are similar to other military organizations, the Corps has managed to distinguish itself by producing a better fighting spirit in its members. Its uncompromising culture that is committed to hard work, high standards, and the unrelenting pursuit of success is evident in all it does.

- The Enron Corporation had a culture that supported innovation, growth, and risk taking—even to the point of cheating. When profits started to fall, many within Enron were addicted to success and sought illegal means to inflate profits falsely. Most leaders resist the temptation of taking or allowing shortcuts in their organization. What an organization believes to be acceptable or unacceptable, ethical or unethical is often derived from what leaders allow or disallow. Leaders are ultimately responsible for what happens in their organizations and as such what they say and do has a profound impact upon the culture of their organizations.

A Happy Place

"Pleasure in the job puts perfection in the work."

—Aristotle

The entire human relations movement, a precursor to the personnel and human resources profession, was based upon this simple and universal truth—"a happy employee is a productive employee." Organizations would be wise to embody this principle.

A series of articles in *Time* magazine on January 17, 2005 were dedicated to the art, science, and mythology of happiness. One article noted that employee happiness is an important factor in performance. *Time* reported that according to Professor Thomas Wright of the University of Nevada, Reno, "happiness could account for ten percent to twenty-five percent of the variance in job performance" for white-collar employees (Thottam, 2005, p. A61). Words such as engagement, authentic leadership, meaningful work, job satisfaction, feeling appreciated, and challenge were littered throughout the article in an attempt to define the conditions that produce a happy and productive employee. The content of the article in some ways mirrors the content of the prerequisites discussed in this chapter. Organizational cultures must support a positive environment, good morale, and a pleasurable work experience.

Changing Organizational Culture

If the environment does not support the desired culture, then the opportune time to start changing it is now. The change can begin with a simple but earnest memo, speech, or conversation with employees to let them know that the leadership wants to make the organization better for all. Culture does not change overnight; in fact, true organizational change takes years. Cultural change within organizations requires numerous deliberate behaviors over a sustained period of time that channel energies and reinforce ideals over and over again. A single act, memo, policy, initiative, pay program, or structural change will not create an ideal culture, climate, or environment.

Good intention alone will not produce change. Just as performance is a series of indicators and evidence, a positive culture is created only by a series of numerous indicators over time. Nonetheless, culture is so important that efforts to shape it are an investment in future performance outcomes.

Culture establishes context. Individual performance occurs within the framework that describes what degree of effort and quality are acceptable and what behaviors are good, bad, or indifferent. Culture regulates norms. Astute managers will make concerted efforts to design, audit, build, redefine, and improve the culture of their departments, divisions, or organizations. Since evidence of culture is not always tangible or measurable, one must study their organization for the many expressions of culture.

Culture is so important that efforts to shape it are an investment in future performance outcomes.

Employee Involvement in Defining and Shaping Culture

What are the fundamentals that are valued, recognized, supported, financed, and disliked? Is performance better or worse in certain departments, branches, or regions? Why? What are the essentials that drive performance in our organization? Are these drivers known or unknown? If they are known, are they positive or negative? If they are not known, or better yet, not aligned with the performance management system, the organization is most likely working against itself. In either scenario, leaders must audit their organizational culture to understand what it communicates and how it affects employees and their performance.

Leaders should not attempt to understand the culture they have created without the involvement of their employees. After all, the employees see the culture more clearly, as they are subject to it. The leaders, by definition, will not immediately see the unintentional effects of their actions, policies, or programs.

If leaders cannot engage employees in meaningful dialogue about the organization and get honest and candid feedback, this is itself an indication of the culture. A poor culture would be an environment wherein employees do not trust managers and leaders enough to be open and honest. When there is little trust, outside consultants may be valuable in helping to solicit such information via surveys, focus groups, interviews, and other appropriate interventions.

Meaningful Work Second

Enriched jobs and supportive work environments motivate people to strive for good performance.
—Benham, "Performance Appraisal: A Radical View," p. 159

The work environment and the work performed are inseparable. How an employee approaches his job every day is a factor of the work tasks and how the employee is treated. The work environment, its climate, and its culture all affect performance. However, the quality of the work being performed also affects how well an employee does his job. Employees need well-defined work tasks in order to do their best work. The characteristics of the work and the work environment that are necessary for solid performance were summarized in Figure 3.1 earlier.

Taking a systems perspective, everything is connected in some way. The work performed, the supervisor, and the work environment can be viewed as one with regard to the employee's work experience. If one of these three elements is negative, performance will suffer.

Managers should not expect employees to do their best work on jobs that do not stimulate their best effort. This argument begs the question, "What if the work is simply not interesting?" One solution to this dilemma is to hire well, as not every job is ideally suited to every employee. Nonetheless, to the extent possible, even mundane and uninteresting work can be made more satisfying through thoughtful work design.

Managers should not expect employees to do their best work on jobs that do not stimulate their best effort.

Work Design

Work design is the art and science of determining what, and how, tasks should be performed and their relationship to other tasks within the organization. Work design involves the tasks themselves, the organizational structure, and the tools and resources utilized in getting things done.

The organizational structure defines who should be hired—and what skill levels and resources are required. The structure of the tasks will affect the level of interest and satisfaction an employee will gain from their work. The level of fulfillment from completing tasks will affect one's intrinsic motivation, and thus their speed, enthusiasm, and commitment to the work. Many experts argue that the more holistic a collection of employee's tasks are, the greater the likelihood the employee will achieve satisfaction from the work. Pride in workmanship is only possible when efforts yield finished products, as opposed to when an employee does one task in an assembly line process.

When mundane, uninteresting, or difficult work cannot be reengineered, then enlarging the job is a potential solution to creating more meaningful work. Job enlargement and job rotation are two options for diversifying work. Job enlargement gives employees more responsibilities in the same job. Job rotation allows employees to do a series of differing jobs to reduce the monotony of routine and repetitive work. Rotating jobs can be set up within a single department or across multiple functional areas. Seasonal rotations, special projects, new assignments, and rotating leadership responsibilities utilize people in such a way as to make work more meaningful.

Regardless of how organizations attempt to make work more meaningful, involving employees in the process is the best method of achieving this goal. Employees will undoubtedly have valuable opinions about what would make their work easier, more challenging, and more satisfying.

Regardless of how organizations attempt to make work more meaningful, involving employees in the process is the best method of achieving this goal.

Employee Involvement in the Design, Delivery, and Evaluation of Work

The employee is a partner in the performance of their work. The employee cannot be allowed to "just do" their job or what they are told regardless of the outcome of their efforts. Employees who focus on putting in eight hours of work versus putting out quality work will be a detriment to any organization. There are countless examples of employees who regularly work doing tasks they know to be inefficient and counterproductive. They feel that they are not compensated for their results; instead they are paid a wage for their time.

One method of cultivating employee engagement is getting them involved in work design. This involvement will stimulate concern for how the work is delivered and build in an automatic quality control mechanism. Employees will understand their work better, know what it takes to track their work, and be able to direct their effort toward producing higher quality outcomes. A fundamental total quality management principle is that quality must be built into the system, not checked after the completed process. Involving employees in the design of their work is the first step in producing quality.

Experts agree that employee involvement is one of the keys to meaningful work and positive outcomes. Employees can make valuable suggestions about how to design and redesign the work they are doing to make it both be more interesting and efficient. In this text, we take employee involvement an additional step further, into the management of the employee's efforts as well. The employee empowerment movement includes quality circles and self-directed work teams. Empowerment has proven to produce a more engaged and productive employee.

Managers Third

[Good managers] build a foundation. These managers realize that the higher the trust level within the office, the easier it is for people to give and receive feedback. They create ways for people to get to know one another, so that feedback sessions aren't meetings between strangers.
—Maurer, *The Feedback Toolkit*, pp. 8–9

Regardless of what performance management system an organization uses, it will only be as good as the manager that utilizes it. Employees do not quit organizations, they quit bosses. How a manager treats employees profoundly effects how the employee views and values the job and the employer. It affects their commitment to the organization and their work. A good manager brings out the best in employees and a poor manager can help to create poor performance and cause organizational turnover. A mediocre manager can unintentionally stifle employees' potential and reduce the organization's chance for future success.

The number one factor employees cite as negatively impacting their work productivity is poor management. Other factors, such as a lack of defined goals and a lack of accountability, may be interrelated with poor management. Training all employees who manage others, as well as monitoring the performance of managers and morale of subordinates, are proactive steps HR professionals can take to improve productivity at their organizations.
—Burke and Esen, *Workplace Productivity*, p. 11

This is precisely why training and developing supervisors is a prerequisite to implementing any performance management system.

All systems fail if the people who work within them do not follow the operating procedures. If an organization creates the best performance management system, it will fail if managers are not properly trained. Unfortunately, we have trained many managers in the time tested but untrue art of Theory X management. Managers are trained to catch employees doing something wrong, versus to "catch them doing something right" (Blanchard and Lorber, 1984) as the one minute manager would advise.

We have created management systems that assume the employee will not do what is best (Theory X); this perspective causes the manager to stay on top of the employee. Managers have been trained to supervise—to be responsible for ensuring the employee does what is required. Instead they should be retrained to coach—to help employees do their best and share the responsibility for output.

Twenty-first-century leaders must build cultures that allow employees to do their best work as well as train and support managers to think differently about performance management. Theory Y beliefs should become the norm and should be reflected in the daily practice of coaching and performance management. Employee involvement and employee empowerment are two good examples of advanced contemporary management techniques. The Performance Conversations® model reflects contemporary thinking on the subject of supervision.

The supervisor-subordinate relationship cannot be adversarial if optimal performance is desired.

The supervisor-subordinate relationship cannot be adversarial if optimal performance is desired. The employee must believe that the supervisor has the employee's best interest at heart, balanced by the needs of the organization. There must be an air of trust among them. The work environment must be built to allow open and honest dialogue.

Trained Managers

Managers must be trained, both in supervision skills and a solid performance management system. Few supervisors ever get formal training on how to lead and manage others. This all too common occurrence is the source of many organizational problems. Organizations spend billions of dollars on training programs each year, but most training is on technical subject matter, not the basics of people management and supervision. Organizations must realize that leadership and management training will far exceed most returns on investments on technical projects.

Regardless of what performance management system is used, all managers must be well trained on the system prior to implementation. For the greatest impact, training must include senior managers. Senior managers, who attended college or business schools decades ago, may practice management techniques that are dated. It is high time for managers throughout organizations to have a uniform perspective about how to work with and manage employees—one that is positive and consistent with organizational norms.

The Manager Title Does Not Equal "I'm Always Right"

Many falsely assume that upon attaining a position of authority they are somehow automatically endowed with greater insights than before assuming such positions. The automatic assumption that the supervisor is right or *more right* than the employee is a great false assumption that undermines solid working relationships. In many organizations, middle managers are well-educated individuals and are often younger than the staff they supervise. A basic assumption in such circumstances is that education is more valuable than subordinate's knowledge and experience. The reality is that a healthy combination of the two is probably preferable to either alone.

Yet in many workplaces, it is "the boss's way or the highway" because the assumption is that the boss is always right. This sort of perspective denies the employees ownership and pride in their work and regards them as if they are not intelligent creatures. If managers are right, that assumes employees are wrong.

> In many workplaces, it is "the boss's way or the highway" because the assumption is that the boss is always right. This sort of perspective denies the employees ownership and pride in their work and regards them as if they are not intelligent creatures. If managers are right, that assumes employees are wrong.

Supervisors Have Only Some of the Answers

A close companion to the idea that managers are always right is the assumption that the managers are the only ones with problem solving skills or solutions. Managers must recognize that employees have a great deal to contribute. This change in perspective must be in place before the proposed performance model can be implemented. The Performance Conversations® model requires the employee's participation and encourages the employee to offer solutions.

Co-Performance

> Clearly employees do not perform solo; they and their managers co-perform and the better the co-performance, the better the results.
> —Bain, "Individual Performance Isn't a Solo Activity," p. 33

Even the best athletes have coaches. A manager can elevate an employee's performance, limit it, or even reduce it. Both manager and employees share responsibility for the employee's performance. Therefore, supervisors must view each performance discussion not as an occasion to hold the employee accountable for their failings, but an opportunity to prevent failure and create future successes. The employee's performance should not be viewed separately from the manger's performance. They co-perform.

Shared responsibility and shared goals are themes in the Performance Conversations® model and are building blocks of a good supervisor-subordinate relationship. "We are in this together; we win or lose together." The manager cannot achieve goals when his employees fail. An unfortunate example of performance management is when the employee does poorly but the manager gets a bonus, or vice versa.

The quality that distinguishes a team from a collection of individuals must be present in managing performance. The team's relationship to one another is larger than the relationship between any of its members. This metaphor is a fitting description of that which must be in place for optimal performance. Synergy is not possible unless there is a mutually beneficial relationship with trust. The manager's training and perception of how to work with employees will affect how employees perform. The manager's false perception may conflict with the idea that the employee is also responsible for performance.

> The employee's performance should not be viewed separately from
> the supervisor's performance. They co-perform.

Employee Involvement and Ownership

Employees who are not concerned about the outcome of their efforts should not be tolerated by any organization. Employees cannot abdicate their responsibility for their effort, their behavior, or their outcomes. An employee who works eight hours and leaves hoping that the supervisor does not discover the work left undone or the mistakes that were made is a detriment to any organization. However, many organizations do not give the employee any reason to assume responsibility for their performance. Many jobs are stripped down to a mechanical view of work, and this perspective robs the employee of pride in workmanship. Many employers ask employees not to think, just to do what they are instructed. Therefore, the employee works a prescribed number of hours without concern for end results. Employee involvement in the design, delivery, and management of their work creates joint responsibility for the outcomes. This is a basic ingredient to success in any work environment. It is also a key element in the Performance Conversations® Model of performance management. Managers must appreciate that the foundation of a successful performance management system is allowing employees joint ownership of their work.

All People Management Systems Aligned—Fourth

Since the performance management system is only one of the systems that manages overall performance, it must be aligned and integrated with all other HR systems to have a true impact on performance. These systems should reinforce one another and support the organization's mission. Here are a few examples of how other HR systems affect individual performance.

Bad Hires Will Likely Create Bad Employees

If we hire the wrong person for the job, it is hard to create the context for the individual to do her best work. This goes back to Deming's quote mentioned earlier: you either "hired them that way, or you made them that way." One method of generating good performance outcomes is to do a good job of hiring people who are best suited for this task. The work is not meaningful if the wrong person is doing it.

Compensation

Employees who are underpaid or not paid commensurate with their peers will value compensation more highly. Frederick Herzberg taught us that compensation is a hygiene factor. When it is adequate, it no longer serves as an important factor in work. However, if it is not adequate, it can have a devastating effect on morale and performance.

Therefore, there is not much an organization can do to create and sustain optimal performance with employees if the organization does not provide its employees with fair, equitable, and adequate pay for the work. It is much harder to ask the employees to take their work seriously if they do not feel valued and compensated fairly. Another simple example of a misaligned compensation system is to reward individual contributions in areas where the goal is for employees to work as part a team.

Training

The training program in an organization must be supportive of performance. Are newcomers oriented to the workplace and given adequate training for the work to be performed? We cannot expect employees who are not fully prepared to perform adequately. When does the employee get formal and on-the-job training? Does it occur before performance problems occur? Are managers supportive of training and development or is time away from work for attending conferences considered "goofing off?" Does the organization require employees to bring back materials from seminars and to share it with their coworkers? Organizational and managerial support is one of the leading indicators about whether an employee transfers learned skills from training to the job (Baldwin and Ford, 1988).

Policies and Procedures

The organization's policies and procedures must be aligned with all other people systems. What does the employee handbook, the policies and procedures manual, the organization's mission, the values statement, and promotional material say about employee productivity? The official, unofficial, and unintentional governing documents should all support the kind of productivity that is desired by the organization. Does the organization state that it encourages employees to take their vacations so that they can relax and renew themselves, but then has a vacation buy-back policy that allows the employee to take a week's salary in exchange for a week of paid vacation?

Is sick leave abuse taken seriously in your organization? If employees see rampant absenteeism go unaddressed, it is difficult for them to take the next productivity initiative seriously. Are retirees treated with respect? Does your CEO frequently discuss enhancing shareholder value but never acknowledge employee contributions? Does your organization pay for country club memberships for executives, but doesn't reimburse managers for membership in their professional associations?

Just as everything the employee does is an indicator of the character and quality of her performance, every signal the organization sends to its employees helps to shape how performance is carried out in the organization. Some of the signals the employer sends are intentional—stated policies and procedures—and some are unintentional. Nonetheless, the organization must be steadfast in its efforts to build the kind of environment that it desires. An audit of its official and unofficial publications and a review of its actions and efforts is a good place to start to make more conscious efforts to manage performance.

Just as everything the employee does is an indicator of the character and quality of her performance,
every signal the organization sends to its employees
helps to shape how performance is carried out in the organization.

Employee Involvement in Performance Management

Employees must be involved in their work to include its entire spectrum, design, delivery, and management. Their involvement will create more engagement in their work and this will likely produce better results.

Conclusion

The key to organizational success is the competitive advantage that comes through the optimal employment of human potential. Managing people is the most important task of any enterprise. How well or how poorly the organization is structured to perform this task may well be the most important factor for business in the twenty-first century. The performance management system is one of the tools for managing performance. The culture of the organization, the quality of the work being performed, the relationship between supervisors and subordinates, and how well human resources systems are aligned and integrated will ultimately affect how well each individual within an organization performs.

The key to organizational success is the competitive advantage that comes
through the optimal employment of human potential.

Quick Reference Points

Chapter 9

- Organizational culture is the most important driver of individual performance.

- Culture establishes norms.

- The primary job of senior management is to create a culture that supports and nourishes individual performance.

- Jobs must be designed to give employees challenge, variety, and pride in workmanship.

- Employees should be involved in the design, delivery, and evaluation of their work.

- Employees perceive their organization through their relationship with their manager.

- Trained and competent managers are a basic requirement for good performance.

- HR policies and procedures must support and reinforce the performance management system and its objective of improved performance.

- The optimal employment of people is the competitive advantage of the new century.

Using the Performance Conversations® Model

The Fabulous Five

Managers must communicate their vision, values, and expectations clearly and create an environment for continual dialogue, while working with employees to ensure they reach their full potential.

—T. Belak

There are five components of the Performance Conversations® approach to performance management:

1. Performance planning

2. Performance log

3. Performance portfolio

4. Progress review

5. Annual Performance Analysis and Summary

In the Performance Conversations® model employees and their managers are in constant communication with one another. They communicate and collaborate in the planning process and in periodic Progress Reviews. They share the responsibility for identifying and tracking performance indicators and they jointly define what is good and bad. Their ongoing discussions give them multiple opportunities to recalibrate efforts as outcomes and circumstances change over time. The manager and employee truly partner for success.

Their success depends on the quality of their performance conversations. Their conversations are based upon the evidence collected by both over the most recent discussion period. The employee and manager discuss work-related issues and give each other feedback. The employee is a co-pilot and full participant in the process of directing and redirecting their efforts. The employee's involvement ensures a degree of engagement, ownership, and responsibility for outcomes. The success of the relationship with the supervisor is to the degree to which the employee and supervisor discuss shared work-related goals and agree on the actions to achieve them.

In the Performance Conversations® model employees and their managers are in constant communication with one another.

Performance Planning

The performance plan is the first step in the Performance Conversations® process. The distinguishing characteristic in the Performance Conversations® process is the degree of participation by the employee. The employee co-owns the entire performance management process.

Performance planning is an ongoing activity, not a one-time event. Performance planning actually consists of numerous plans happening at various stages of completion, action, inaction, design, and conception. Every performance conversation is part planning, discussion, adjustment, analysis, and discovery. Planning occurs at every stage of the process. New plans are constantly developed to respond to new information, facts, awareness, or opportunities.

Performance planning involves a discussion of expectations, standards, and goals. When planning is completed well, the parties agree on the roles, responsibilities, and time lines. Agreement is the key variable. Performance planning is an active process and the employee is a major player.

The distinguishing characteristic in the Performance Conversations® process is the degree of participation by the employee. The employee co-owns the entire performance management process.

Planning is Active

Performance planning can be likened to action learning and action research. In action learning, the individuals involved learn from one another. They learn by doing and by constantly analyzing and reflecting upon the process in which they are engaged. It is a sophisticated and ongoing process of discovery that is driven by hypothesis generation and hypothesis testing. The individuals iden-tify a problem, create a possible course of action, test their ideas, evaluate the results, and then repeat the process.

Planning is only a starting point. Adjustments are always required when reality and plans converge. The response options are to continue with the plan, stop the plan, or adjust the plan. Regardless of the conclusion, planning con-tinues. As in most performance management systems, a plan precedes actual performance. In our system, the individual is involved at each stage of the process.

Employee Involvement in Planning

First, the employee's input is given equal credence with the supervisor's in the Performance Conversations® model. The plan requires negotiation between the supervisor and employee to determine the scope of work and necessary action steps. After all, the employee is the one who will actually have to complete the work tasks, so understanding and agreement are mandatory.

Second, the employee enters the planning process prepared. The em-ployee is not allowed to abdicate responsibility for planning since it is a pre-cursor to the successful execution of work tasks. Therefore, planning that is conducted by the supervisor alone is incomplete. To borrow a common business phrase, "If the employee is to be in on the landing, then he or she must be involved in the takeoff." The employee must come to the planning process having analyzed the job's requirements and their past contributions to participate fully in forecasting future efforts.

It is preferable for the employee to write down bullet points for discussion at the planning meeting. If the employee attends a Performance Conversation® unprepared, it is advisable to reschedule the discussion to give the employee the opportunity to prepare. The employee cannot be a bystander in their own performance management.

> The employee is involved in performance planning and the employee's input is given equal credence with the input of the supervisor.

Third, since the employee is going to have more responsibility for ensuring the plan is executed, she must fully understand the plan and the success criteria. The employee must recognize the indicators that prove the plan is working as intended. As the employee has been heavily involved in designing and develop-ing the plan, the employee will have more ownership and a greater degree of responsibility for execution. Employee involvement allows fewer excuses for poor performance and reduces the likelihood that poor performance will be an issue.

Fourth, the goal of planning is for the employee and the manager to agree on work tasks. If the employee is involved in, contributes to, and understands the plan of action, it will be far easier for the plan to unfold successfully. A degree of quality control is built into performance because the employee will also understand how to recognize good performance. Agreement symbolizes understanding. The employee knows what is to be accomplished and his or her role in executing the plan.

> In the Performance Conversations® model, we assume a Theory Y view and that the employee is trying earnestly to do all the things that are expected.

When describing the employee's role in the planning process, it can be summed up in a single word, *engagement*. The employee co-owns overall performance, so planning must be a process shared between the employee and the manager. The Performance Conversations® process employs the employee's sense of ownership, investment, and responsibility.

> If the employee is involved in, contributes to, and understands the plan of action, it will be far easier for the plan to unfold successfully.

Planning in the Performance Conversations® model occurs formally and informally. The employee is involved in developing short-term, long-term, and annual performance plans. Their plans are aligned with those of the organization and they are responsible for common goals and responsibilities. Discussions about progress made, problems identified, or adjustments needed are required parts of these structured Performance Conversations®.

Summary of Elements for Performance Planning

- Employee involvement
- Employee preparation
- Discussion, negotiation, and agreement
- Ongoing, evolutionary process
- Formal and informal, short- and long-term plans
- Multiple plans occurring simultaneously

Performance Log

[E]ncourage employees to maintain notes about their performance. Consider requesting employees to make self-assessments of their performance.
—Johnson and Kaupins, "Keeping Lies Out of the Performance Appraisal,"
pp. 4–6

The Performance Log is a detailed list of indicators that describe the character, quality, and quantity of performance activities, efforts, behaviors, and results.

The Performance Log is a detailed list of indicators that describe the character, quality, and quantity of performance activities, efforts, behaviors, and results. It is a collection of small, large, notable, minor, mediocre, incidental, routine, formal, and intangible indicators of performance. The Performance Log is not intended to analyze or interpret performance, but simply to make note of it. It does not summarize, it reports on performance.

The log can be any device or instrument used to record performance. The Appendices include several sample logs. The Performance Log documents things that appear mundane as well as those that appear important. The recorded note can simply be a word, a phrase, a sentence, or a paragraph about past performance. The goal is to document performance in real time. The preference is for the record to be simple, quick, and easy.

Examples of Performance Logs could be a collection of sentences written on Post It® notes, paragraphs kept in a spreadsheet, a bulleted list of activities maintained on a computer, notes kept in a journal, or a few sheets of paper listing things observed. The goal is to record any and all performance activities. Logs are best when they are simple.

The goal is to document performance in real time.
The preference is for the record to be simple, quick, and easy.

Employee Involvement in the Performance Log

[E]mployees possess valid, unique, and relevant performance information and insight that is unavailable or unobservable by the rater.
—Roberts, "Employee Performance Appraisal System Participation," p. 2

The Performance Log in the Performance Conversations® model is actually two logs, one kept by the supervisor, and one kept by the employee. The employee is present one hundred percent of the time and will therefore have observations that the supervisor will not see. Since the idea of the Performance Log is to record as many indicators of performance as possible as they occur, both the employee and the supervisor are involved in the "logging" of performance indicators.

The supervisor keeps notes of employees' contributions that are observed or communicated. The supervisor documents attendance, work progress, behavior, compliments, complaints, extra efforts, mistakes, corrections, conversations, and any other item of interest or concern deemed noteworthy.

The Performance Log in the Performance Conversations® model is actually two logs, one kept by the supervisor and one kept by the employee.

The employee tracks their own work, capturing and monitoring key performance indicators. The employee logs items that the supervisor does not see or experience. The employee can toot their own horn by highlighting a job done well. The employee records how they felt when confronting a major challenge, documents challenges with coworkers or other departments, and identifies obstacles to superior service. Noting performance obstacles is particularly important, as these notes will be shared with the manager. The employee records anything that he or she feels is pertinent to his or her work and performance.

Since dialogue is the primary ingredient in the Performance Conversations® model, it occurs throughout the process. One of the greatest advantages of conversations using Performance Logs is that the employee and the supervisor discuss actual work elements. Lively conversation about the differences and similarities in the two logs is inevitable. Differences of opinion about what was recorded and what is important are critical to clarifying what is expected and required to produce good results.

Performance Logs also facilitate a 360-degree look at performance.

Performance Logs also facilitate a 360-degree look at performance. The employee and the supervisor can record information received from all sources. Thank-you notes from customers or complaints made by coworkers can all be recorded in the Performance Log for future conversations. When information and perceptions from others are recorded for discussion, it does not mean that the perception is accurate, only that someone has the perception. The Progress Review is a great opportunity to validate what others have said or done and why such perceptions exist.

Sample Models of Performance Logs

> Managers can collect performance data . . . based on written documentation such as diaries and critical incidents.
> —Johnson and Kaupins, "Keeping Lies Out of the Performance Appraisal," p. 4

There are numerous ways to keep a collection of notes; in fact the possibilities are endless. What managers and organizations should avoid is insisting upon a "one size," "one instrument," or "one method" fits all approach. Every job is different, and the tool used to track performance should be appropriate to specific jobs and employees. The type of log used by nonexempt employees might be different from that used by exempt employees.

Here are some examples of the approaches to logging performance:

1. A *spreadsheet* with one row used for each entry (performance indicator).

2. A *collection of loose-leaf sheets of paper* used to record activities, events, and results.

3. A *calendar* with notes written on days when a worthy indicator of performance occurs.

4. A manila *folder* with a series of sticky notes or papers attached—each note documenting a performance event.

5. A series of *short summaries* drafted by the manager and/or employee of the employee's activities. These can be generated daily, weekly, or as needed. There are at least two popular approaches to using summaries.

    • The seven-by-seven method: The subordinate is asked at the end of a week to write down things done over the previous seven days and to forecast their plans for the coming seven days.

    • The fifteen-by-five method: The subordinate spends no more than 15 minutes documenting their recent performance; the summary should take no more than 5 minutes for the supervisor to read.

6. A *journal* kept by the employee and/or manager.

7. A *notebook* with pages divided by tabs, one section dedicated to each employee reporting to a manager.

Regardless of the methodology used in the Performance Conversations® model, the Performance Log should be populated in real time. It should be brief and factual, and there should be two Performance Logs, one recorded by the employee and one by the manager. Appendices I–IV offer four different examples of ways to track performance.

Elements of Performance Logs

- Detailed list of indicators: efforts, activities, behaviors, outcomes, results, etc.

- Activities recorded in real time

- Continuous documentation

- Simple, factual records

- Big and small items: significant and seemingly insignificant items

- Operational, work-related items

- Employee records indicators: includes feedback for supervisor

- Manager records indicators

Performance Portfolio

Portfolios provide a format for collaborative and systematic collection of data for reflection and analysis, development of professional growth plans, and verification of progress towards individual and program performance standards. This form of assessment includes both formative and summative information, addresses how individuals reason and engage in problem solving and creates a forum for facilitation of communication among colleagues that includes reciprocal feedback processes (Knight and Gallo, 1994, p. 66).

The Performance portfolio is simply a collection of performance indicators. The collection includes Performance Logs, documents, reports, records, results, samples, examples, notes, awards, and any other evidence. It is a storehouse of information that contains the result of various data collection activities. The contents of the Performance portfolio will vary according to the job being performed, even for employees doing similar work. It is evidence of work planned, attempted, or completed. In short, the Performance portfolio is a repository of all information. Appendix V contains a checklist of sample portfolio contents.

The Performance portfolio is a collection of Performance Logs, documents, reports, records, results, samples, examples, notes, awards, and any other evidence.

How Do You Know the Employee is Doing a Good or Bad Job? Prove it!

One of the problems with traditional performance management systems is that they commonly rely on summaries. What is included in the summary determines the characterization of performance. The summaries may gloss over or completely omit important information. Normally, there are only a handful of indicators noted in the summary, only those observations made by the supervisor. The Performance Portfolio alleviates this issue by being a repository of information collected by the employee and manager. It also contains both general and specific performance information. The Performance Portfolio contains more than a *sample* of performance; it contains *examples* of performance.

In contrast to the Performance Log, the Performance Portfolio includes everything that one can put in a file folder or container. It is a collection of the evidence of performance and the Performance Log is a part of its contents. Items such as results, tabulations, sales numbers, quarterly reports, or other documents are included. The beauty of the Performance Portfolio is that it is an assortment of information that attempts to describe fully the performance and performance context. Anything and everything that describes an individual's contributions should be included. Therefore, when it is time to discuss the performance, all meaningful information is available at the manager's and the employee's fingertips. This reduces the chance of an employee disagreeing with the manager's assessment of their contributions since all information is known and open for interpretation. The Performance Portfolio is a version of instant feedback; all the available information that characterizes the employee's performance is available at anytime.

360-Degree View

The Performance Portfolio also offers the opportunity to collect multiple sources of information and a 360-degree look at the position and performance. Input from customers, coworkers, professional associates, and vendors should be included in the portfolio. Information from top management, subordinates, or others is fair game. The greater the number of performance indicators collected from different sources, the richer the information will be as a basis to make interpretations about performance.

Employee Involvement in the Performance Portfolio

The Performance Portfolio can be maintained either by the employee or the manager, but there should only be a single Performance Portfolio.

The Performance Portfolio can be maintained either by the employee or the manager, but there should only be a single Performance Portfolio. The employee should have unrestricted access to the Performance Portfolio at all times and should be encouraged to review its contents frequently. It is positive that the employee would want to review the contents of the Performance Portfolio at various stages during the year to reflect upon their performance. Thoughtful reflection is a likely precursor to deliberate improvements.

Both the employee and the supervisor should review contents of the Performance Portfolio prior to and during each progress review.

Both the employee and the supervisor should review contents of the Performance Portfolio prior to and during each progress review. After each progress review, the most recent Performance Logs will be deposited into the Performance Portfolio as will other indicators of performance. The employee may deposit an e-mail compliment received from a coworker or a photocopy of a completed report. The supervisor might contribute a leave balance statement that shows the pattern of paid time off taken, or a handwritten note indicating that the employee's exceptional efforts in the most recent sales campaign. The Performance Portfolio could also contain a photograph of a new product created by the employee.

The Performance Portfolio should be a dynamic file, with contents added daily, weekly, monthly, or as appropriate.

The Performance Portfolio should be a dynamic file, with contents added daily, weekly, monthly, or as appropriate. The file should, of course, be held confidentially by either the employee or the manager.

Elements of the Performance Portfolio

- Performance logs
- Reports, statistics
- Results

- Evidence

- Awards and thank-you notes

- Specific and general items

- Everything that describes the performance

- A living file

- Data collection

- Multi-source feedback

- Confidential material

- Access and reflection is encouraged

Progress Reviews

During the year, it is important that you evaluate your employees frequently, giving plenty of feedback about their performance. One approach is to set "mini-evaluation" sessions periodically throughout the year. At these sessions, simply exchange perceptions about performance under each responsibility on the pie chart. Listen to the employee's perceptions and paraphrase his or her points of view, attempting to clarify the differences, if any, concerning actual performance versus desired performance (Robinson, 1995, p. D-4).

> Progress reviews are periodic, semi-formal, non-evaluative discussions about the content of Performance Logs and Performance Portfolios.

Progress reviews are periodic, semi-formal, non-evaluative discussions about the content of Performance Logs and Performance Portfolios. They are the occasions to make adjustments and plan for short-term tasks and performance. These occasions create an opportunity to step back from the work to reflect on progress. Some organizations refer to them as "check-in sessions."

All experts agree that feedback should be an ongoing process. Progress reviews are the basic building blocks of effective performance management. They occur every four to ten weeks and create the occasion for feedback to be exchanged. While there should be daily and weekly feedback shared, progress reviews ensure that more structured and detailed feedback is shared at least every four to ten weeks. For more senior positions, however, once a quarter may be reasonable; for certain very junior positions, every other week might be an appropriate meeting schedule. Once a progress review is scheduled, a manager should honor the schedule. A change of time or date may send the message that there are more important things than the employee. If employees are our most valuable assets, they should be treated as such.

Structured, Planned Opportunities for Discussion

Progress reviews are semi-formal because they can be planned and they are required. Planned reviews should be placed on the calendar to occur at regular intervals. Progress reviews can also be impromptu when there is downtime or when a natural break occurs. When progress reviews are unscheduled, the employee and supervisor should take time to collect their notes and materials and update their Performance Logs. The conversation will be based upon the records and evidence of performance, not memories. Progress reviews are formal in that there are a prescribed part of a performance management system and informal in that they are not regimented in format, length, or methodology. These sessions are designed to be free-flowing discussions about all things pertaining to work events and tasks that have occurred since the last progress review. Once the two parties are accustomed to the periodic reviews, they usually will last from fifteen minutes to a half-hour (Drumm, 1998).

Progress reviews are semi-formal because they can be planned and they are required.

The style of progress reviews is situational. Sometimes they contain an agenda, sometimes they are brainstorming sessions, and sometimes they are simply chances to recognize an employee for excellent performance. Progress reviews are non-evaluative because the goal is not to label or rate the performance, but instead to describe, discuss and analyze the most recent performance. Progress reviews also validate the data collected. They do not lay blame, but, instead troubleshoot obstacles to outstanding performance.

The discussion of work events or tasks could be as simple as, "We tried A, B, C, and D over the past few weeks," or "Let's talk about how things are going!" "Plan A is going well, lets continue it. Activities B and C are not meeting our expectations, so let's make some adjustments." And, "Our reports do not appear to have enough information about what is going on with D. What should we do about D?" Progress reviews are great coaching sessions.

Progress reviews are great coaching sessions.

Bad news is not avoided, but discussed for agreement and understanding. The analysis necessary to achieve an understanding of the problem becomes the basis upon which solutions are derived and challenges confronted.

If things are not going well, the supervisor should give specific feedback regarding what has not gone well, elicit from the employee their understanding of the problem, and come to a mutual agreement regarding how to best address it. If things are going well, the supervisor should give specific feedback regarding what went well and why.

—Laurel, "User Friendly Performance Management," p. 5

During progress reviews, part of the conversation is dedicated to adequately describing past events and future plans. The information in the Performance Log and Performance Portfolio become the basis upon which open, honest, and candid dialogue is built. The supervisor and the employee start from the same point. Next, the two agree upon what the information collected means or implies. The ideal scenario is that there is agreement on all conclusions drawn and interpretations made.

Bad news is not avoided, but instead it is discussed for agreement and understanding. The analysis necessary to achieve an understanding of the problem becomes the basis upon which solutions are derived and challenges confronted.

Once an agreement is reached, the next step of the progress review is to enter the planning cycle again. In formulating a course of action, there are three important questions to ask: (1) What are those things that we should continue doing? (2) What are those things that we should stop doing? (3) What are those things that we should do differently? This is the opportunity to make corrections and adjustments and to recognize and reinforce successes. As stated earlier, if agreements cannot be reached after earnestly trying, *ties always go to the manager.* "Improvement in performance usually results from progress reviews—not end-of-the-year summary reviews" (Drake, 1998, p. 36).

If agreements cannot be reached after earnestly trying, ties always go to the manager.

In Real Time

Progress reviews occur in real time—as performance is occurring, not months later. This allows for early interventions into performance problems. More importantly, it creates the opportunity to reinforce success. Progress reviews facilitate discussion about standards, activities, and results. Feedback about efforts and outcomes is exchanged in real time; feedback is not delayed until questionable results are noticed.

Progress reviews occur in real time—as performance is occurring, not months later.

Real time discussions allow supervisors to monitor what is going on and have the opportunity to change the approach as necessary. According to Drumm (1998), such discussions also allow time to address extenuating circumstances related to performance, allowing priorities to be adjusted and resources to be reallocated as appropriate.

Shared Responsibilities

> If the manager keeps canceling scheduled meetings, for example, he or she is held accountable if goals are not met. If an employee is promised a project planning session, but the manager keeps postponing it, the subordinate may not be able to continue without the manager's support, and should not be blamed if the project fails.
>
> —Bain, "Individual Performance Isn't a Solo Activity," p. 34

Both employee and manager are responsible for the employee's performance. Performance Conversations® give them the opportunity to focus and align their collective efforts. The underlying question in the relationship is "What can we do better together?" An underperforming employee may speak poorly of the manager's ability to supervise and of the performance of their department. Because their fates are inextricably tied, the Performance Review is the prime occasion to work together. Due to their suggested frequency, progress reviews create six to ten planned opportunities each year to collaborate on performance improvement. Partnerships that are designed to troubleshoot and problem solve are forged during these sessions.

Both employee and manager are responsible for the employee's performance and they share the common goal of improved performance.

Employee Involvement in Progress Reviews

The employee is an equal partner in the progress review and should be engaged in reviewing the data collected over the past few weeks. The employee should respond to the relative weight of the positive indicators in comparison to the negative indicators. The employee does a self-assessment of his or her efforts and also comments on the support and guidance received from the manager.

The manager should not dominate the conversation. It is a vital element of the Performance Conversations® approach that the employee is active and engaged. Therefore, managers work best in this model when they ask questions and solicit the employee's opinions instead of providing the answers.

It is a vital element of the Performance Conversations®
approach that the employee is active and engaged.

Employees should be asked to interpret the information collected in the Performance Portfolio to assess performance and he or she should be asked how the manager could have better supported their efforts. The employees' answers undoubtedly yield rich information for discussion and illustrate their level of understanding and expectation. The employee should be required to offer suggestions, solutions, and alternative ways of working on the issues presented. Their ideas must be taken seriously.

The manager is an active listener in the progress review. The employee must be given an opportunity to talk and offer information. Employee involvement should not be *pro forma*, it should be legitimate and a necessary ingredient for two-way *conversation*. If the employee has not kept a Performance Log, not tracked their performance, or reflected upon recent progress, the progress review will be incomplete and inadequate. Part of the manager's responsibility is to ensure the employee is tracking and logging their performance. Appendix VI provides a checklist of the items that should be a part of a typical progress review conversation as well as guidelines for conducting an effective session. Appendices IX and X can be used by the supervisor and subordinate to stimulate discussion about overall performance. They contain a series of sample performance questions and ideas to consider.

The Performance Conversations® model demands co-performance,
which claims that an employee can only be as good as their
supervision, support, and guidance.

The employee should be expected to give feedback to the manager. The Performance Conversations® model demands co-performance, which claims that an employee can only be as good as their supervision, support, and guidance. Therefore, a key question for the manager to ask the employee is, "What can I do to help you achieve better results?" The manager may be able to supervise the employee differently, allocate more resources, support the employee differently, assist the subordinate with certain tasks, or strive to give clearer instructions.

Ask employees what you can do to make their jobs easier, better, and more meaningful. This step is probably the most neglected aspect of the . . . process, yet their answers can make all the difference. Indeed, you may find that you are part of the problem when you should be part of the solution.

—Day, "A Hard Look at Performance Reviews," p. 3

At the conclusion of the progress review, the employee or the manager should write a simple summary of the interpretations made and the plans agreed upon for the next four to ten weeks. It is also a good idea for the supervisor and the employee to rotate the responsibility of writing the summary. After all, it is a partnership and employee participation is essential. Brevity and simplicity are important. The summary could be in outline or bullet form with only enough information to be accurate. Appendix VII provides two sample progress review summaries.

Summary of the Progress Review

- Scheduled, every four to ten weeks as appropriate for a given job

- Semi-formal process

- Discussion and dialogue driven: two-way communication

- Review of plans, logs, and portfolio.

- Operational, problem solving, and troubleshooting activity

- Description and agreement of issues, challenges, and successes

- Adjustments, corrections, negotiations

- Ends in agreement

- Manager also receives feedback

Annual Performance Analysis and Summary

The summary is used to dissect and diagnosis past performance problems; the analysis is used to determine how to best proceed in the future.

The annual performance analysis and summary is the formal occasion when the manager and employee discuss the content of the progress reviews (Performance Logs, Performance Portfolios and the notes from the Performance Reviews) and create a shared summary of the year's efforts. The goal is to agree upon what is important, why it is important, and plan for the future.

Properly conducted, it cultivates a shared responsibility—co-ownership. This analysis and summary are focused on the future and are not linked to compensation. It contains at least three elements: (1) an analysis of performance information collected over the previous period, (2) a summary of important trends, (3) and an opportunity to restart the process of planning for the future. The annual performance analysis and summary (APAS) is a planned event.

By virtue of the fact that the APAS is a summary, it has a historical component. It is a review of all work tasks and events that have occurred to date. It is an overview of each Performance Log, the Performance Portfolio, and each progress review. All indicators of performance are available for scrutiny. The Performance Portfolio is studied and the examples of performance are examined. the progress review notes are carefully reviewed. Each of these elements should raise questions, cause discussion, and yield some degree of understanding and appreciation of the past year's activities.

Before the APAS session begins, the employee and the supervisor must have reviewed all materials collected. The review of all data and information is the basis of the discussion. If the data gathering process (Performance Logs) is taken seriously and progress reviews are conducted in earnest, there should be no new information introduced at this stage of the process. Now performance can be viewed as a whole in addition to its parts.

If the data gathering process (Performance Logs) is taken seriously and progress reviews are conducted in earnest, there should be no new information introduced at this stage of the process.

The year in review should provide a different perspective about performance from any one period of time. The whole should be more meaningful than the sum of the parts, and the APAS provides the occasion to identify larger issues, patterns, and trends. The only thing that is new to the APAS is the macro-level interpretation of the year's performance. This interpretation can include comments about behavior challenges. Idiosyncratic behaviors emerge as patterns over time and are seldom obvious when they occur, so the APAS creates the opportunity to acknowledge and address patterns. More severe behavior challenges that directly interrupt work performance should have already been addressed in progress reviews.

The APAS is also the occasion to be strategic, to ensure that efforts are aligned with the mission, values, goals, and initiatives of the organization. It is different from progress reviews, which tend to be more operational. The APAS deals with the "why" in addition to the "what" of performance. It is also the final opportunity for quality control since it is the opportunity to compare last year's plans with what was actually accomplished.

New plans are developed for the coming year. Goals and objectives are set and agreed upon, and action plans are developed. These action plans will be discussed and tracked at each progress review. Appendix VIII provides a checklist and guidelines for conducting an APAS conversation.

Search for Shared Meaning, Understanding, and Purpose

One of the goals of the Performance Conversations® process is for the supervisor and subordinate to seek agreement on the characterization of performance. When the two share the same understanding of what needs to be done and how it is to be accomplished, their joint efforts are channeled in the right direction. These performance discussions are powerful because synergy emerges from collective thoughts and actions.

Since the APAS is strategic, one of the topics discussed can be shared purpose.

Since the APAS is strategic, one of the topics discussed can be shared purpose. It is an opportunity to continue relationship building. The optimal result is that the two agree that they are on a common quest, and that they share the same purpose and goals—excellent performance. The ideal is that they both agree to work together better, renew faith in each other, and rededicate themselves to their common cause. These agreements recognize their shared responsibilities.

Future Oriented

Focus on the future. The purpose of most performance appraisals is to improve performance—in the future. Get off past events as quickly as possible, and discuss ways you can work together in the future.
—Maurer, *The Feedback Toolkit*, p. 55

Because the APAS is not attempting to label or rate past performance, it can be more optimistic in tone. Regardless of how well or marginally an employee has performed in the past, the APAS is a chance to create an ideal future without yesterday's baggage. The summary is used to dissect and diagnosis past performance problems; the analysis is used to determine how to best proceed in the future. The purpose of the planning activities in the APAS process is a call to action and a chance to calibrate efforts. Each of these activities focuses attention and efforts forward, not backward. The process is intentionally called an analysis and summary instead of a summary and analysis; the focus is on performance *improvement,* not Performance *Review.*

The process is intentionally called an analysis and summary instead of a summary and analysis; the focus is on performance improvement, not Performance Review.

Renewal and Recognition

The APAS is an opportunity for renewal. It can serve as a collective *pat on the back*. If the results from the previous period were satisfactory, then the employee and the supervisor can revel in the occasion and reflect upon a job well done. It is a time to reinvigorate oneself, rededicate to the challenges at hand, and renew commitment to work together for the future.

Individual Development and Career Development

The Performance Conversations® model does not include a career development component as a part of its framework. It is preferable that the individual's long-term developmental activities be separate from near-term operational matters. Individual development plans should be done at another time, as it is focused on individual growth not the specific work activities discussed in detail in Performance Conversations®.

Employee Involvement in Annual Performance Analysis and Summary

The employee's involvement in the annual performance analysis and summary is the same as it is in progress reviews. The employee is an equal partner engaged in the process, and their input is necessary and meaningful.

The employee co-owns performance and co-owns the performance management process. The employee will be called upon to explain or interpret the information collected. The employee must be involved in describing what happened and in diagnosing problems, as the employee will have to implement the remedy for bad situations. Therefore, the employee must be crystal clear on the issues at hand and in agreement with plans to improve performance.

The APAS is also the right time to discuss the employee's job description and how their role fits in with coworkers and the overall department. As noted earlier, it is also the time to ensure that the employee's efforts are aligned and support the mission of the organization.

While there is some attraction to having semi-annual analysis and summary sessions, the use of periodic progress reviews eliminates the need for semi-annual formal sessions. Feedback should be ongoing and periodic, casual and formal. The combination of daily, weekly, and monthly supervisory feedback with progress reviews and an annual performance analysis and summary session should create more than sufficient information to manage any job. Appendices

IX and X provide a list of questions and ideas to consider that help the supervisor and subordinate prepare for the annual discussion.

Elements of the Annual Performance Analysis and Summary

- Employee and manager review Performance Portfolio prior to APAS

- Review the summaries from each progress review

- More strategic than operational

- Analyzes past content

- Does not contain any new information other than a macro interpretation of performance

- Determines if big changes or small adjustments are needed

- Provides recognition, as appropriate

- More focused on performance interpretation than on operational problem-solving

- Aligns efforts with organization mission, initiatives, and goals

- Review job description, etc.

- Sets goals and plans for future shared responsibilities

- Yearly event

The Performance Conversations® Model Summarized

The Model Step-By-Step

The steps in the Performance Conversations® model are straight-forward. The employee and the supervisor have numerous structured and planned opportunities to meet to discuss operational and work-related matters.

Performance Plans: The employee and manager meet to discuss standards and expectations and to make both short-term and long-term plans for the coming year.

Performance Logs: The employee and manager individually document performance indicators as they occur in separate Performance Logs.

Performance Portfolio: The employee and manager gather documents or other evidence of performance and put them into a folder.

Progress Review: The employee and manager meet every four to ten weeks for a *check-in* to discuss the contents of the Performance Logs and Performance Portfolio. At this time, they share feedback, make adjustments, and discuss progress on goals.

Annual Performance Analysis and Summary (APAS): At the end of the year, the employee and manager meet again to interpret (*analysis*) all of the content of the Performance Portfolio and Performance Logs to determine trends, patterns (*summary*), or other discoveries.

The key to success is open communication at each juncture; two-way communication and feedback. The richness of communication comes from the fact that the conversations are about the evidence of performance that both parties have collected. The frequency of conversation ensures that efforts are coordinated, that activities are monitored, and that outcomes are tracked.

Small Investment, Gargantuan Return

Eight progress reviews—Performance Conversations®— of a half hour each is only four hours a year, and is a small investment for great outcomes.

Sitting with each subordinate eight times a year—a progress review every six weeks—for a half hour to discuss performance issues may at first seem like a management burden. But it is a small *investment* for improved performance. Overall performance improvement is one part good supervision and one part solid performance management process. The Performance Conversations® model incorporates activities that the manager should have otherwise been performing:—monitoring and regulating performance of subordinates. Second, the model is as much preventative as it is proactive; it prevents performance from getting too far off track since it constantly recalibrates efforts. It also has a multiplicative effect on good performance as it acknowledges good efforts and seeks to replicate them.

Eight progress reviews—Performance Conversations®—of a half hour each is only four hours a year, and is a small investment for great outcomes. Any manager who is too busy to make a small deposit should not expect a return. Managers get what they expect as they monitor and track ongoing efforts in Performance Conversations®. The constant dialogue ensures that the employee is given feedback as soon as possible, so there are no surprises. Problems are addressed sooner, successes are reinforced, and opportunities are seized. The communication, collaboration, and coordination inherent to Performance Conversations® create the ideal conditions for excellent performance to occur.

A New Approach Based upon Structured Opportunities for Dialogue

---

Dialogue is the absolute foundation of performance management.

The Performance Conversations® model requires new and different, rather than traditional, approaches to performance management. While some of the shifts in thinking are subtle, others are profound. The involvement of the employee is not a new concept, but the degree to which the employee is involved is significant. This increased involvement cannot happen if the *Prerequisites* to good performance management are not in place.

Dialogue is the absolute foundation of performance management. The employee and the managers are equally invested in a quest to discover all the indicators of performance. They talk openly about issues and come to agreements. A review of past performance is important as a means of understanding it; however, the goal of the review is not to label performance or to lay blame. Rather, the goal of the review is to assess conditions in order to chart plans for future success.

Performance Conversations® are structured opportunities for feedback built upon problem-solving dialogue between supervisors and subordinates that are designed to calibrate and recalibrate work efforts. Supervision techniques are integrated with performance management tools, forming two sides of the same coin. Their aim is to improve individual performance. Performance Conversations® focus on the future with the goal of creating and replicating successes through the use of co-performance where the supervisor and subordinate work together to create positive outcomes.

Quick Reference Points

Chapter 10

- Performance Conversations® are operational, work-related discussions.

- The model is future oriented and non-evaluative.

- The employee and supervisor have multiple opportunities to talk and solve problems.

- They both gather performance data; all the indicators of performance (efforts, behaviors, and outcomes).

- They each maintain a Performance Log.

- They create a folder—Performance Portfolio—to hold all the evidence of performance that they have gathered.

- They share information, give one another feedback, and negotiate options.

- They agree upon options, and put them into play.

- They meet frequently to calibrate and recalibrate their joint efforts; they co-perform.

- They communicate, cooperate, and collaborate.

- The name of the game is feedback; the sooner it is shared, the better it is.

- They hold an annual Performance Planning meeting.

- Every four to ten weeks, they discuss the contents of their Performance Portfolio and Performance Log during a Progress Review conversation.

- Problems are addressed at this Progress Review; good efforts are reinforced, and recognition is given.

- At the end of the year, they study the evidence of performance gathered and discussed over the year to uncover positive or negative trends. The results are used to plan for the next year.

- As long as the two take advantage of the many structured opportunities for discussion, they can work together to create success.

PART IV

Pay Considerations

The salary that an employee commands conforms to a variety of social and personal facts. The use of performance appraisals as a basis for salary changes concentrates only on the perception of the employee's performance, disregarding all the other facts. Among the factors affecting an individual's salary are: market rate, responsibilities, skills, education, prosperity of the company and the community, seniority, individual performance, and all other personality traits. The complex combination of these facts determines what the employee will be paid.

—Hans D. Allender

The Fallacies of Pay and Pay Alternatives

A FULL ANALYSIS OF compensation matters is beyond the scope of this book. However, critics will argue that performance management and compensation are so inextricably tied that you cannot discuss one without the other. Indeed, many of the misuses of performance management systems are attributable to using money as a management control mechanism. A cursory explanation of the common problems and challenges with compensation are offered here. A few preliminary solutions to these common mistakes are also given.

Once you embrace the twenty-first-century approaches to management offered in the Performance Conversations® model, you will also want to get a twenty-first-century understanding of the do's and don'ts related to pay matters. Most authorities on the subject advise that performance management systems must be decoupled from pay systems. This is good advice as these systems have difference purposes.

Pay systems are designed to recruit, retain and motivate individuals to perform. Because performance appraisal systems are designed to document and record *past* efforts, there is a natural disconnection with traditional systems. Performance management systems are designed to track, monitor, manage, and document performance with the goal of improving performance. The misalignment of such systems places unnecessary pressure on the supervisor to direct attention toward the right things.

Using pay to manage performance is based upon economic models which do not acknowledge that human behavior is more complex than a simple financial transaction. Politics, personal preference, fear, favoritism, jealousy and other human tendencies all affect performance and they all complicate the simple carrot and stick incentive model that forms the basis of most pay-for-performance or merit based systems. Like the many Fallacies of Appraisal, the

Fallacies of Pay are also doomed to fail before they are used in performance management.

Fallacy E explained why pay is ineffective at motivating performance. Money tends to attract attention away from the performance it is trying to affect. This chapter identifies some troublesome pay practices that managers should avoid when attempting to manage performance. It also provides some potential solutions for organizations which aim to take a more progressive approach to partnering with their employees for mutually beneficial success.

> Using pay to manage performance is based upon economic models which do not acknowledge that human behavior is more complex than a simple financial transaction.

Pay Fallacies

Money Can't Buy Me Love

One of the major assumptions of this chapter is that money can buy labor, but it cannot buy commitment, loyalty, or affection (love) for the work or the organization. Most organizations approach money matters in a way that is self-defeating. The trust of employees for their employers is undermined when the organization does not honor its word or hides portions of the truth about money. In these circumstances, money is not used as an exchange for labor, but as a tool for control. The idea that one is being controlled or manipulated with money does not create meaningful or mutually beneficial relationships with employees.

> Money can buy labor, but it cannot buy commitment, loyalty, or affection (love) for the work or the organization.

Tell the Truth about Money

An organization should share with employees its approach to compensation; if not, it will cause some to be suspicious. If coworkers discover that some positions are paid more than theirs without any justification, they will not be happy. When employees do not know *why* or do not understand the organization's policies, it breeds an atmosphere of suspicion and distrust. These feelings create a very negative work environment, reduce loyalty, and lower morale.

It may be a competitive disadvantage for organizations to provide employees (and competitors) their compensation philosophy, policies, and practices. However, at the minimum, employees should understand the approach so that it is not secretive or assumed to be random. Employees who believe that they are not being paid fairly will likely believe that they are not being treated fairly.

A major part of telling the truth about money is to help educate employees about basic compensation science. The most important concept about compensation that should be communicated is that organizations establish pay rates for *positions*. This practice limits how much organizations are willing to pay individuals who work in those positions.

Compensation 101

How most organizations pay their employees is based on supply and demand. It is simple capitalism. As a matter of fact, most organizations attempt to pay individuals as little as possible for their labor. This is evidenced by the fact that pay rates for most organizations are based upon the supply of labor in a given geographical area. A company may pay fifteen dollars per hour for a bookkeeper in an urban area, but pay only fourteen dollars for the same position in a rural area. One may ask why the company does not pay fifteen dollars for both or fourteen dollars for both. Organizations only pay enough to attract the amount and kind of labor they seek, and seldom anything more. This typical practice is used to remain competitive and create shareholder wealth.

Compensation is based upon the value of a particular kind of labor in that particular marketplace and is not based on the value of the individual providing the labor. A nuclear physicist who works as a custodian will earn the typical wage of a custodian. She may do the job particularly well and therefore earn a higher than average wage, but the wages will be bound by the typical range for that type of labor in the marketplace.

This very important principle is not usually understood by employees. This phenomenon is often played out by the administrative assistant who goes to night school to earn a bachelor's degree. Then the employee demands more money from the employer, only to find that the employer does not give him a wage increase. The individual is then insulted as he has demonstrated that he is more capable now (and presumably "worth" more), but is not being compensated for the new potential. The truth is that the salary paid will be for an administrative assistant, not a college graduate. If this same individual applies for a management trainee position, then the salary paid will be commensurate for that particular position.

In summary, pay is based on supply and demand. The going labor rate is usually expressed as a dollar range in a particular geographical area. Within these defined dollar ranges, novice employees earn at the bottom of the range and veteran or excellent performing employees tend to earn at the top. The range is specific to the position and the type of labor performed and does not commonly vary based on the person performing the tasks.

For many positions, a pay range of forty to fifty percent is typical. Therefore, for the bookkeeper position noted above, most people who perform that job nationwide would earn between twelve and eighteen dollars per hour. Even the best bookkeeper is likely only to earn eighteen dollars per hour. A particular bookkeeper might perform so well that an organization would be willing to pay twenty dollars per hour, but that would be a rare circumstance. Even a person who was honored as Bookkeeper of the Year would likely never earn thirty-five dollars per hour as a bookkeeper, even if he or she had thirty years experience, held three master's degrees, never made a mistake, and could do the job of two bookkeepers blindfolded. The typical practice in organizations is to hire three bookkeepers at twelve dollars an hour rather than pay a very good bookkeeper thirty-five dollars per hour.

Pay Is Always Limited

Organizations pay for labor by the position, not by the person. Commonly, when an individual's compensation increases to the point that it is outside of the normal pay range, most organizations take efforts to limit the individual's pay progression.

If the bookkeeper's compensation increases to nineteen dollars per hour, which is outside of the pay range of twelve to eighteen dollars per hour, many organizations will take steps to limit compensation. The organization then does one of several things: (1) give the employee more responsibility, (2) give the employee additional work, (3) reduce the annual percentage increase as compared to their peers, (4) give a bonus increase versus a percentage increase so that the additional pay is not compounded over time, (5) simply stop giving the employee increases, or (6) promote the employee to another job with a higher pay range. Regardless of how an organization chooses to deal with this issue, it reinforces the principle that organizations pay for positions, not for the people; compensation is not based solely on the value of an individual's contributions. This startling fact stands in complete contrast to all incentive compensation.

Incentive compensation implies that an individual has a seemingly endless opportunity to earn more income. The reality is that this endless opportunity does not exist in many organizations, since at some point their compensation will hit the upper limit of what the organization is willing to pay. Pay is limited because the organization could presumably find others to do similar work for a substantially lower amount of money.

Compensation is not based solely on the value of an individual's contributions.
This startling fact stands in complete contrast to all incentive compensation.

The Economy and Profitability Affect Individual Compensation

In traditional systems, many factors beyond employee control affect compensation. If an organization is performing well, it can afford to pay employees better. However, when an organization has a bad year, it reduces its merit pool, thereby lowering each individual's potential earnings. Basic pay, merit pay, and incentives are affected by an organization's ability or desire to pay. In good economic times, x degree of effort yields a y amount of bonus or merit compensation. However, in poor economic times an *x-plus-one* degree of effort may yield only a *y-minus-two* amount of bonus. This reality undermines the effectiveness of any incentive plan.

Equity Theory

Equity Theory has two components and they are both related to fairness. Do I believe that I am paid fairly as compared to others within the organization who do similar work? Do I feel I am paid fairly as compared to those outside of the organization who do similar work? Or put another way, "Am I, the bookkeeper, paid reasonably in line with accountants down the hall and bookkeepers and accountants at similar companies?"

Organizations violate the principles of equity theory in at least three ways. First, companies that do not explicitly explain how they pay employees leave it open for speculation. Second, organizations claim to pay for performance and then do not offer a significant differential in pay for poor performers in comparison to excellent performers. The excellent performers will be de-motivated if they find that a 25 percent better effort only produces a two-percent difference in annual increases.

Third, organizations tend to reward all employees when the organization is doing well. This may unintentionally undermine both equity and expectancy theories. When employees notice that their good efforts are worth less at times and the less notable efforts of others are worth as much or more, they stop responding to incentives. This is particularly discouraging for stellar performers who see weaker performers benefiting handsomely, despite their marginal efforts.

If an organization is performing well, it can afford to pay employees better.
However, when an organization has a bad year, it reduces its merit pool.

Stockholders Are More Important Than Employees

Organizations do not typically share profits with employees. The leaders of modern corporations are obligated to the shareholders for financial outcomes, not their employees. This is not to be critical of publicly traded companies; it is a simple fact. Many corporations treat their employees poorly in bad economic times; some even treat them as if they were disposable. Organizations layoff or dismiss employees regardless of how well the employees have performed in the past. Sadly, many are released regardless of how many years of service the employee may have with the corporation.

Fortunately, not all organizations have such brutal and uncaring practices and lack of concern for their employees. A good example would be Southwest Airlines. Southwest did not lay off employees after the 9/11 tragedy; they reinvested in their employees and were profitable in 2001 and all subsequent years. Other airlines told thousands of employees on September 13 and 14 not to report back to work, as they were being laid off. Many were informed via the telephone and even voicemail.

It is difficult for employees to be committed to an organization that appears to have only one concern, "What have you done for me lately?" If organizations treat employees like disposable resources that can be bought and sold at a moment's notice, then managers should not be surprised that they must cajole, manipulate, force, or trick employees into working harder. The relationship an organization has with its employees is the foundation of good performance.

If employees do not trust the organization, or if the employee is afraid of losing their job at a whim, they are not likely to be committed to the goals of the organization. If employees feel that they are only there for the financial benefit of the stockholders, they are not likely to be engaged employees.

If organizations treat employees like disposable resources that can be bought and sold at a moments notice, then managers should not be surprised that they must cajole, manipulate, force, or trick employees into working harder.

Non-Profits Pay Less

Non-profit organizations typically pay less than for-profit organizations on average as they have fewer resources. Secondly, non-profit missions tend to be philanthropic, or for the common good. Leaders of these organizations are being good stewards of the resources entrusted to them when they pay only that which is necessary and nothing more. To some degree, non-profits expect their employees to believe in the mission first and view their labor, in part, as a contribution given toward helping to fulfill the organization's mission. Non-profits do not compete for talent in the labor marketplace with wages; instead they emphasize the social capital of their mission. They also accentuate their benefits package, and most often they provide greater challenge and opportunity for employees. These factors help non-profits attract employees who are motivated by the greater good more so than a pursuit of riches.

Balancing the Budget

According to experts, all compensation programs are designed to attract, retain, and motivate employees. But the important caveat is that it must be *within the organization's ability to pay.* Therefore, wealthier organizations tend to pay more than those with fewer resources. Presumably, more profitable organizations can afford to pay a higher wage and attract better-qualified employees.

However, the caveat is significant and restricts an organization's ability to do all that it may want to do. Organizations have to balance profitability, reinvestment in the business, and give employee compensation. This is also a reason many incentive plans fail. If an organization claims that it *pays for performance* and everyone performs well, they either reduce the amount of merit compensation all individuals can earn or they reduce the number of high performers who can receive the incentive. After all, the compensation manager has to work within a budget.

Furthermore, the amount of merit compensation an employee will receive is often based on the performance evaluation rating. If managers inflate ratings, they create an additional financial obligation *for* the organization. Organizations then have to redefine what "good performance" is financially worth in order to balance the budget. Redefining the value of "good" after the performance has occurred or redefining because of a reduction in profitability violates the principles of expectancy theory. Does the employee believe that they will get the promised reward, regardless of company budget or profitability? Employees will lose faith in the organization's statements regarding compensation if the company does not do what is promised. The performance of employees who lose faith in their organization's commitment to the truth will decline, or worse, employees may choose to leave the organization.

Percentage Increases Disadvantage Lower Paid Employees

A marginally performing mid-manager who earns $84,000 per year is given a two-percent pay annual increase for lackluster performance. An outstanding customer service associate who produces double that of peers earns $26,000 per year and in recognition of his stellar performance is given a six-percent raise. However, the math reveals that the middle manager will take home an additional $1680 and the hardworking customer service associate will only gain an increase of $1560 additional dollars. Due to the use of percentages instead of flat rate increases, the organization either misplaces rewards or sends confusing signals to employees about organizational values. Percentage increases also prove that organizations do not pay for performance.

> Pay is usually a symptom that other things are not going well. When employees complain about pay, they are usually indirectly indicating that they are not happy with their work situation.

Pay is Usually a Symptom, Not a Cause

Pay is usually a symptom that other things are not going well. When employees complain about pay, they are usually indirectly indicating that they are not happy with their work situation. Pay is a lightning rod issue as it is more tangible than poor management and lack of appreciation. Research shows that this phenomenon also exists within unionized organizations, where pay is not the most important reason employees seek to join unions.

Poor pay is seldom the root cause of unhappy employees; it is usually poor treatment and poor management. An example, "What would happen if an employer with a morale problem gave all employees a fifteen percent increase in pay?" Morale would likely improve for about a month. After the initial excitement, the root causes of the problems will resurface and there would be no net gain in morale.

More Reasons Why Incentives Fail

While money is important to employees, what tends to motivate them to perform—and to perform at higher levels—is thoughtful, personal kind of recognition that signifies true appreciation for a job well done. Numerous studies have confirmed this.

—Nelson, *1001 Ways to Reward Employees*, p. xv

Hygiene and Motivators

Frederick Herzberg stated more than fifty years ago that money was only a hygiene factor. It has been proven over and over that money does not motivate behavior for any sustained period of time. However, the absence of basic fair compensation is indeed a de-motivator. Disregarding this reality, those who advocate the use of incentives claim that all it takes is a little money, and all will be well. The use of incentives and motivation theories that use money as their basic tool for managing human behavior are misguided. Money as a tool for management is the source of a great deal of poor performance.

The problem with incentive and motivation theories is that they are based upon an economic model. In the twenty-first century we know that economic models do not account for all human behavior. Incentives will not persuade individuals to do the right things all of the time.

The problem with incentive and motivation theories is that they are based upon an economic model. In the twenty-first century we know that economic models do not account for all human behavior.

Expectancy Theory

The Expectancy Theory of motivation is based on the belief that if one works harder, one will get a greater reward. The assumption is that the employee actually values the reward offered and reasonably expects to be rewarded as promised. This theory is documented in compensation texts, but seems to be ignored by compensation system experts.

The use of incentives is undermined in that employees might not value the incentive offered. The employee may not be willing to work to get the reward for a variety of reasons. Here expectancy theory is highlighted to illustrate one additional point—as stated, it is predicated upon the *belief* that *if* one works harder, one *will* receive a greater reward. So, all incentives are based upon the idea that if Jane works harder than Bob, Jane will receive the greater reward.

A problem with the use of incentives is that organizations are not consistent in their "guarantee" to employees. This is best illustrated in times when an organization is highly profitable and good performers get six percent raises and the poor performers get three percent raises, yet in bad economic times, the good performers get three percent raises and the bad performers get one percent raises or no raise at all. It is not an effective incentive for good performers to work all year not knowing whether they will get three percent or six percent. Good performers' "belief" that they will collect the incentive they expect is undermined if the organization fails to deliver the expected incentive only once. Incentive systems are undermined when individual incentives are based on factors the employee cannot control.

Bean Counters

One of the most damaging mistakes made when rewarding employees is when a senior, HR, or compensation manager downgrades the award or merit increase a manager recommends for a subordinate. A manager regards Sue's performance as outstanding and recommends she be given two days off with pay, but the central office thinks that the meritorious service for which she is being recognized is worthy of only one day off. While the manager should wait for approval before sharing the nomination with Sue, it is still a disincentive for the manager to nominate any employee in future. The action questions the manager's judgment, even though only the manager observed the performance.

When managers are overruled it sends the message to staff members that the organization may not support the manager's assessment and their performance is not valued as highly. It also reintroduces Expectancy Theory. The individual is not sure if the rewards earned will actually be given as the authority of their manager is undermined. Therefore, all raises, merit increases, or incentives are questionable.

What Would You Do For a Million Dollars?

To prove further the point about the fallacy of incentives to affect human behavior over a sustained time period, consider this proposition. Imagine the difficult task of working overseas for one year without any contact with family or friends. Would you consider a job that paid you twice your current salary with these conditions? If you said "yes," now after being paid two times your salary, would you stay a second year for four times your normal salary? Many would not accept the first proposition. Even those that would take the first proposition may not accept the second.

What is your value of one million dollars? Would you spend a year away from your family for one million dollars? Would you stay a second year for an additional million dollars? At some dollar value, all individuals will stop being motivated by an ever-increasing amount of money; this is evidence that money is a hygiene factor, not a motivator.

Many incentive systems are based upon the false assumption that there is only a small percent of resources available to employees. The truth is that the amount of resources available is to a great degree determined by managers.

False Scarcity of Resources

Many incentive systems are based upon the false assumption that there is only a small percent of resources available to employees. The truth is that the amount of resources available is to a great degree determined by managers. Managers could usually increase the amount available if they wanted or needed to do so (within the limit of their ability to compete in the marketplace and their profitability). One example of the false scarcity of resources is when departments are given a set percentage of resources, based upon payroll, to reward employees annually. If the manager has four percent to distribute, giving six percent to one person means another person may have to get two percent or less. This policy of using a percentage of payroll does not acknowledge that certain departments might deserve an average of eight percent raises, while others might deserve an average of six percent or three percent.

Such polices undermine supposed compensation policies that employees are compensated fairly and or that state that "we pay for performance." In many situations, organizations could, in reality, afford to allow certain departments the discretion of giving six percent or eight percent average increases. Instead, it is far easier to administer an across-the-board merit program. It is also less expensive for the bean counters who determine how little they will reward employees and how much profit is passed along to shareholders.

Recognize System Effects on Individual and Vice Versa

Many factors beyond an employee's control affect compensation. Many organizations give raises, bonuses, and merit pay based on performance of a particular product, geographic area, or market. It is unfair to employees to claim that their efforts will determine their compensation when in fact their compensation is determined by the performance of their department, supervisor, organization, or even the economy.

Success Without Incentive Pay

Non-profit organizations thrive despite paying below market rates. Government employees do work for the public good and collect average wages. Research has proven that union employees are more productive on average than non-union employees although collective bargaining agreements do not normally provide incentives or individual pay differentials. Consider that members of the military and many small companies are paid the exact amount for the jobs they do without any pay variance to individuals. Consider also the wages of clergy and employees of various religious organizations. These are just a few examples of situations when differential compensation is not used to attract, retain, or motivate individual performance. Compensation theorists do not talk much about these situations; instead they base their theories on the sexy environment of multinational corporations and other big organizations. The truth is that a few incentive pay plans make the headlines, but few are actually in place and even fewer actually have a positive long-term impact on performance.

The truth is that a few incentive pay plans make the headlines, but few are actually in place and even fewer actually have a positive long-term impact on performance.

Summary: Labor Is for Sale, but Commitment and Engagement Are Not

Organizations may use compensation to persuade individuals to join, or even affect individual performance, to a certain degree. However, loyalty and commitment are not for sale. Incentive pay is of limited value in improving performance; fair and equitable pay is a requirement.

Pay Solutions

Below a certain echelon of management, the amount of money most employees can earn is limited. There is no denying that money rewards have motivational power. What is not well understood, however, is just how limited financial rewards by themselves are in developing the kind of emotional commitment that builds the long-term sustainability of any organization, whether for-profit corporation, nonprofit, or government agency. Money by itself is likely to produce self-serving behavior and skin-deep organizational commitment rather than the type of institution-building behavior that is characteristic of organizations like the Marines, the Home Depot, and Southwest Airlines.

—Katzenbach, *Why Pride Matters More than Money*, p.1

Organizations should first and foremost seek to hire individuals
who believe in the organization's mission.

Shared Beliefs and Goals

Organizations should first and foremost seek to hire individuals who believe in the organization's mission. Individuals who have passion about the organization's mission or products will have an evangelical spirit and a sense of purpose, and will perform better than individuals who do not share similar beliefs.

Treating people fairly, with dignity, and with a sense of importance will create an environment of mutual trust, admiration, and respect. Shared beliefs and goals will engender a positive spirit of cooperation and collaboration. These factors alone may produce good performance, but without a doubt they create the opportunity for good employees to work together toward shared goals.

This idea is common for many non-profit organizations. In community organizations that promote the arts, you are likely to find many artists on staff as administrative assistants, project managers, and directors. These employees care about advancing the arts and have aligned their belief system with their vocation. They are not financially motivated or interested in self-gain. They seek to make a fair wage and do good work for a good cause. If an economic model is the basis for how work with others is defined, both sides will attempt to maneuver or negotiate the best terms and conditions for themselves to the disadvantage of the other. If taking advantage of the other is considered getting a good deal for oneself, their future together cannot be bright.

Open Up the Books

It is easy for organizations to be coy about how much money they are making in good economic times when they are sharing the fruits of prosperity. But in times of poor profits or economic uncertainty, employees are more skeptical and employers are usually less generous with compensation. By not sharing certain economic information in good times and in bad, organizations create an air of distrust with employees.

The Container Store and many other companies have found ways to share financial information with employees to the degree necessary for them to understand the basis for organizational decisions. Understandably, it is difficult to make information available when competitors might take advantage of the data, but just enough information can be made available to make decisions transparent. Publicly traded companies might educate employees about the meaning of their financial statements and explain how finances relate to the corporate strategy. Employees should understand how the building of buildings, the entry into new markets, advertising costs, lagging sales, the economy, layoffs, and low raises are all correlated. If employees do not understand, they will create their own assumptions. Communication is key—employees who want to understand are brighter than we give them credit for being.

Market Pay or Better

> There is a baseline of monetary need and "fairness" beneath which motivation and pride will sink. When people are not paid enough to meet their fundamental human-safety and comfort needs, neither pride nor loyalty prevails.
> —Katzenbach, *Why Pride Matters More than Money*, p. 18

When it comes to actual compensation, any for-profit company that wishes to maintain good talent should pay at least an average market wage. Paying lower than market wages and then using incentives to allow employees to earn more money sends mixed and misdirected signals. Paying a good wage, a market wage, says that the employee's contributions are valuable. All other programs and policies related to pay are inept if the company does not pay a fair market wage.

Non-profit organizations may lag the average market wage and still maintain a good market position. It is assumed that non-profits compete on the basis of their mission and other intangibles. Nonetheless, non-profits should also strive to pay competitively with other non-profits. When possible, leading the market with pay or paying a wage that is appreciably higher than competitors also sends a message to employees. It says that the organization believes that only through good employees does it advance its mission. This should be a goal of organizations that can afford this luxury.

Leading the market with pay, or paying a wage that is appreciably higher than competitors also sends a message to employees. It says that the organization believes that only through good employees does it advance its mission.

Recognize, Recognize, Recognize

Studies indicate that employees find personal recognition more motivational than money.

—Nelson, *1001 Ways to Reward Employees*, p. xi

Recognition is a consistent finding in any research about employee happiness, job satisfaction, motivation, and performance. Genuine appreciation is the best reward. A manager that understands the employee's work tasks and has a positive relationship with the employee is likely to create an environment that nurtures good performance. Recognition is formal acknowledgment. The manager may express appreciation as a matter of practice, but recognition makes it conscious, overt, and tangible.

A consistent practice of good feedback is a half-measure toward recognition. Positive and negative feedback are both forms of recognition. Even employees who perform poorly want attention so that they can be guided toward good performance. This is a postulate of Theory Y thinking. Recognition in public is well received by many. Formal ceremonies, plaques, names posted on bulletin boards, public announcements, a firm handshake, an informal gathering at the end of the day, an e-mail, and many other activities can be used to recognize employees. The primary goal of recognition is the formal expression of appreciation. An employee who does not feel appreciated will not perform their best.

Pay is a form of recognition. However, it can never be the only or the most important element of an organization's recognition program. Expressing the depth of an organization's appreciation for contributions in terms of dollars is fraught with potential problems. Since more money is never enough, pay recognition can devalue the intent of the recognition.

In the absence of recognition, many employees seek a pay increase as a way of demanding recognition and acknowledgment of their efforts. They want someone to notice that they are doing well and for someone to say "Good job" or "Thank you." Yet, we should not lose sight of the one important management axiom, that appreciation is recognition. This is echoed by Marcus Buckingham (Buckingham, 1999), author of *First Break All the Rules,* when he notes that the most effective recognition program is regular supervisory feedback.

Rewards should be tokens. They should be provided after performance has occurred; never as payment for performance, only in recognition of it.

Rewards

Rewards should be tokens. They should be provided after performance has occurred; never as payment for performance, only in recognition of it. Rewards should not be expressed as incentives, or as a *quid pro quo* arrangement. Rewards should not be promised or expected, otherwise they lose their value. Paying employees poorly and offering rewards can be viewed as only making the employee whole, not offering any gain.

There are countless ways to reward employees; taking tips from Bob Nelson's book on *1001 Ways to Reward Employees* is an excellent place to start (Nelson, 1994). A final principle with regard to rewards is that rewards should occur as close to the notable performance as possible. Waiting until the annual raise cycle to give a reward for performance is too late. Rewards are like feedback and should be given as close to the event that is being rewarded as possible.

Awards Instead of Rewards

Dictionary definitions of the words "awards" and "rewards" reveal a clue as to how tokens of appreciation should be distributed. Rewards are considered something given to compensate someone for doing specific tasks, such as finding a lost article or completing work. Awards are things that are granted for special efforts or that are deserved due to merit (Websters, 2001, p. II). Taken literally, rewards are things that are earned and therefore cannot be considered *additional* compensation, appreciation or recognition. Therefore, awards are viewed as acknowledgement and rewards can be viewed as payment.

The spirit of awards is more consistent with a Theory Y mindset. Recognition programs should offer tokens of appreciation after performance has occurred in recognition, not in exchange for the performance. So, technically speaking, the use of the term *awards* would be a better descriptor of how organizations should acknowledge and celebrate employee efforts. However, regardless of the language used, good performance should be celebrated after it has occurred. Carrots should never be used to create false motivations for good performance.

Good outcomes should always receive attention. However, sometimes good efforts that fall short should be recognized as well.

Recognize Outcomes, Efforts, and Behaviors

Supervisors and organizations should recognize employees for supporting organizational goals. Good outcomes should always receive attention. However, sometimes good efforts that fall short should be recognized as well. Behaviors that support good performance should not be overlooked. The sports metaphor of the "most improved player" or the "best team player" awards exemplifies the idea that there are other reasons to recognize performance than just outcomes.

A Proposed Rewards Protocol

Inevitably, pay will be used as one type of reward, but it should be used consistent with the principles mentioned above. Organizations should allow managers to give "On-the-Spot" awards. These rewards are almost impromptu as they occur at the discretion of the manager and at a time closest to when the exemplary performance occurred. Some contemporary use of "On-the-Spot" awards is giving gift certificates, movie passes, flowers, and other non-cash awards as tokens of appreciation for noteworthy employee actions.

A use of on-the-spot awards that would be consistent with the ideas expressed in the Performance Conversations® model would be to give managers the authority to give on-the-spot raises and on-the-spot bonuses. What would be more powerful in influencing repeated good performance than a manager bringing attention to those things that the organization seeks to reinforce and rewarding immediately?

> Research by Dr. Gerald Graham throughout the United States revealed that the type reward employees most preferred was personalized, spur-of-the-moment recognition from their direct supervisors.
> —Nelson, *1001 Ways to Reward Employees*, p. 3

To ensure that the on-the-spot awards are not used in a manner inconsistent with their design, they should be limited to some defined amount of money and limited to a small percentage of potential recipients.

Managers should be given complete discretion on awarding them, but must be able to justify to their superiors why they gave such rewards. The reward happens when and how the manager decides, without review. However, the manager's pattern of giving awards should be reviewed by Human Resources and the manager's superiors. If the manager uses rewards and awards incorrectly, the manager should be retrained or disciplined, but their subordinates should not be denied.

All awards and rewards, including financial awards, should be administered fairly. Managers must make difficult decisions and reward only those most deserving. To do otherwise will undermine any performance system and destroy relationships with employees. Finally, awards can be given to groups to reinforce teamwork.

Reward Teams If People Have to Work Together

Most compensation systems are designed around individual compensation. In contrast, most work assignments require people to work together. One solution is to abandon individual incentive compensation systems in favor of group compensation systems. Profit sharing, employee stock ownership plans, and "gainsharing" are some methods of addressing this challenge.

Gainsharing is a profit sharing concept for the non-profit world, but it has universal application. It designs systems that allow groups who produce good outputs to receive some reward or "gain" for their efforts. A simple example of gainsharing is giving an entire department a day off for doing a good job. Increasing a department's budget, allowing a team to use work time to develop new products, or increasing annual raises after the organization successfully lowers its operating expenses are other examples.

In all circumstances, such reward systems should not produce winners and losers on the same team. Managers should not put team members in the position of competing or working against one another to receive an award. Awards should reinforce and recognize cooperation and strong teamwork.

Most compensation systems are designed around individual compensation. In contrast, most work assignments require people to work together.

Encourage Employee Ownership

For-profit corporations should encourage employee stock ownership. It would be ideal for there to be a benefit that facilitated or even subsidized employee stock ownership. Employee ownership will nurture pride in the organization's products. Employees who view themselves as owners will likely invest more than their time into the organization.

Inflation and Market Adjustments Are Mandatory

All employees should receive an annual increase that mirrors inflation to ensure that employees do not lose ground in the actual value of their compensation. Periodic reviews of employee pay should occur and the pay for appropriate positions should be adjusted by market-based increments, as appropriate, to maintain external equity. If the labor marketplace increases the wages of wrench-turners, the organization should pay market wages, regardless of how they have performed as individuals. The goal here is to ensure that all employees within the organization are paid fairly as compared to the labor market. With these prerequisites in place, then other pay-related programs can be successfully implemented.

Organizations should celebrate their heroes. It is in an organization's best interest to communicate with employees the type of behavior and outcomes that it values.

A Proposed Merit Pay Plan

Organizations should celebrate their heroes. It is in an organization's best interest to communicate with employees the type of behavior and outcomes that it values. Organizations that recognize their employees will produce better performance than those who do not. It is also a good idea for an organization's compensation practices to be aligned with and supportive of the organization's mission, goals, and initiatives. When employees are clear on what the organization values and then those things are rewarded, positive performance will follow.

Organizations should publicly announce how much money they will provide to employees in the form of merit. If merit is true merit, then the number of employees who can be nominated to receive a merit award should be limited to no more than fifteen percent of employees each year. Supervisors (and in some circumstances coworkers) should nominate deserving employees by writing a letter of no more than two pages with the reasons why a certain employee deserves meritorious recognition.

The nominated, the nominators, and the meritorious letter should all be published organization wide. The documents will illustrate to the entire organization how managers and leaders judge meritorious performance. These documents will serve as examples of what others should emulate. It may be necessary to keep the actual names of nominees confidential; every organization will have to determine where the line between prudence and privacy should be drawn within their organization.

Each employee nominated should receive appropriate recognition and some token for their nomination. The organization should then distribute the entire pool of meritorious pay to those nominated. The awards, and where possible, the amounts should be announced to the community as well. This approach will help the organization instill the correct "organizational behaviors." Due to public scrutiny, abuse will be reduced, and all the right behaviors, efforts, and outcomes will be acknowledged by all.

Decisions regarding who should receive an amount of meritorious pay should be made by a committee. The committee members should be known to all employees, though their deliberations must be confidential. The committee should include an executive, a middle manager, a rank and file employee, an HR professional, a financial representative, and others as necessary. The lively debate about what efforts are valued and most important to the organization should help to create solid organizational policies and communications.

Organizations should publicly announce how much money it will provide to employees in the form of merit.

Pay, Rewards, and Awards in Review

Several ideas have been offered to redefine how performance can be compensated and managed in the twenty-first century. All ideas work together and more importantly, reinforce one another. They are consistent with the Performance Conversations® model of performance management and help to create a positive environment wherein excellent performance can occur. Many of these ideas are already practiced in many organizations, but the important differences offered here create a new framework for the practices to be used with the greatest impact.

A shift in thinking is necessary to change how we approach performance management and how we treat, manage, and pay people. Paying a competitive market wage, aggressively using recognition, offering employee ownership options, and using gainsharing is a great start for organizations to create the optimal conditions for employee performance to flourish. However, tying these programs to performance appraisals will doom them to failure. Therefore, the approaches to pay in the Performance Conversations® model are not directly linked—they reinforce one another, but they are not defined by one another.

Paying a competitive market wage, aggressively using recognition, offering employee ownership options, and using gainsharing is a great start for organizations to create the optimal conditions for employee performance to flourish.

Quick Reference Points

Chapter 11

- Do not use economic models of human behavior to manage employee performance.

- Money can buy labor, but not commitment.

- Always pay at least a market wage; leading the market would be better.

- Give inflationary adjustments each year.

- Review compensation periodically and make appropriate equity adjustments.

- Many, many organizations are successful without using incentive pay.

- Hire people who are passionate about the organization's mission and purpose.

- Recognize. Recognize. Recognize.

- Non-financial rewards should make up the predominant part of the reward program.

- Reward groups instead of individuals.

- Reward outcomes, efforts, and behaviors.

- Give awards to deserving employees—not everyone; make tough decisions.

- Celebrate performance heroes publicly.

- Merit pools should be discussed openly.

- Encourage employee ownership.

- Separate pay policies and Performance Conversations®.

PART V

Final Thoughts

Objective by objective we have discussed the limitations of performance evaluation in the framework of the TQM organization. Moreover, the perceived benefits can work against the company. Consequently with the TQM principle that customers are paramount, it's invalid to ask what benefits customers receive from performance evaluations. The bottom line shows that performance evaluations do not make any contribution or add value to customers. On the contrary, the system squanders money that could be used in better ventures. Only one action fits performance appraisal systems. Get rid of them.

—Hans D. Allender

Conclusion

PERFORMANCE APPRAISALS ARE RELICS of management systems gone bad in the twentieth century. Enlightened organizations and those of the future will redefine their relationships with their employees. Enlightened organizations will not use performance appraisals and incentives in an attempt to control and manipulate employees but provide employees with a rich and meaningful work environment that supports success.

> High performing organizations of the future will have one thing in common—they will treat employees well.

The Competitive Advantage of the Future

High performing organizations of the future will have one thing in common—they will treat employees well. Before ordinary organizations can transform themselves from good to great, they will have to make a shift in what they know and believe about people management.

If managers have a Theory X perspective, nothing can be done to produce a high performing organization, because the employees will not give their very best performance to an organization that does not deserve their very best. It has been said that organizations can buy labor, yet they cannot buy commitment, loyalty, or trust from employees. Passion is not given to organizations that are only interested in organizational gain—endlessly higher profits at the expense of those who help to produce them. Employees of the twenty-first century will not commit their professional lives to employers who might dispose of them at will because of one unprofitable quarter.

The relationship between the employee and manager will be a partnership. Supervision cannot succeed in an adversarial framework where employees and management are out to take advantage of one another. Organizations will work hard to create the right environment for their employees' success and expect them to participate fully in the process of building and maintaining a better workplace.

Twenty-First-Century Models of People Management

In the twenty-first century, we must have new models to manage performance. Using models such as coaching, partnerships, co-performance, and employee engagement will ensure that human capital is valued and treated appropriately. Regardless of what model we use, simple dialogue—two-way communication—is the indispensable criterion upon which work relationships will be built and thrive. *Communication*, *cooperation*, and *collaboration* should become buzzwords that help to define new generations of employee-manager relationships.

Keep Talking: Conversations Pave the Way to Future Success

"Can we talk about this?" Psychologists, counselors, and mediators alike agree that if there is difficulty involving two or more people, the path to a resolution is healthy discussion. Open and honest discussion—whether negotiation, diplomacy, or conflict resolution—are necessary for mutual satisfaction. Conversations are important to problem solving at work and are fundamental ingredients in performance management. The Performance Conversations® approach is built upon this universal idea.

Performance Conversations® Model in Review

The Performance Conversations® model is an important management advance in that it returns performance management to its rightful place: day-to-day tasks and responsibilities that are synonymous with supervision. Managers and employees share responsibility for creating and replicating good performance. Managers and employees maintain dialogue, work together, and partner to find solutions to common challenges. They co-perform. The Performance Conversations® model cultivates positive relationships built upon dialogue, trust, and co-determination.

> Join the new millennium and leave the appraisal in the past.
> —Coens, *Abolishing Performance Appraisals*, p. 6

Use these tools to propel yourself and your organization to a new level of performance and reap the benefits of a happier, more productive work environment. Best of luck to you!

Quick Reference Tips

Chapter 12

- Performance appraisals are old management technology.

- The competitive advantage of the future is the optimal employment of human potential.

- Organizations should work hard to create a positive and nurturing environment for employees; this allows natural human potential to flourish.

- The employee-manager relationship should be closer to a partnership.

- Other important metaphors that describe a twenty-first century approach to supervision are coaching, co-performance, employee involvement, and engagement.

- Communication, cooperation and collaboration are the new buzzwords to describe how managers and employees should interact with one another when working toward positive outcomes.

- The Performance Conversations® model integrates performance management with supervision.

- The Performance Conversations® model creates structured opportunities for dialogue that builds relationships, trust, and positive outcomes.

Appendix I

Sample Performance Logs
(Spreadsheet)

Subordinate's Log

		Ivan Goode	
	Date	**Performance Indicators** January–March 2006	**Remarks**
	1/7	My year-end reports were submitted today.	
	1/27	I successfully closed on the sale of a new version of ERP software with two existing clients. The sale was made in December but the check came today.	I wonder if this counts towards my fourth quarter totals?
	1/30	Quarterly reports shows that I had third highest totals company-wide	
	2/1	Updated the contact list of all 2005 leads	
	2/10	Completed my review of the specifications for beta tested 2007 models	
	2/10	Attended an online seminar of the "Art of the Close" selling technique	
	2/15	Sold three new Version 8 models	
	2/16	I made 20 cold calls today	
	2/18	I'm having trouble getting reimbursements paid on time from accounting. It is discouraging for salespeople who travel often to have delayed reimbursement checks. My credit card bill may be past due as a result.	Talk with Susan about this.
0	3/1	Vacation scheduled March 1–5	
1	3/8	Have draft contract in hand for two upgrades. Tried technique learned in the online seminar and it appears to have been effective.	
2	3/8	I was pleased to get a thank you note from Mary Victors. She really likes using the new products we sold her in February. She says that her revenues are up.	
3	3/9	I was late submitting the proposal outline. It was due 3/1. I know that I should have prepared the report before I left for vacation.	
4	3/11	Bi-monthly progress review scheduled	

Supervisor's Log

		Employee name: Ivan Goode	Prepared by Susan Henderson
	Date	**Performance Indicators** January–March 2006	**Remarks**
	1/05	Ivan called in sick, after the long holiday break.	
	1/27	The Executive Search Company purchased more Acme products. Ivan was the lead on this sale.	
	1/30	Ivan's sales revenues are impressive again as noted on the quarterly report.	Copy of quarterly report shows Ivan's skill as a salesperson.
	2/10	Ivan offered very good comments to the software developers on the roll out of the new beta version. Good salespeople know their products. Ivan knows his products and his diligence in reading the specifications is an indicator of his serious approach to work.	
	2/15	Ivan was kind to assist Roger Smith with the proper method of using our new sales tracking software.	
	2/18	I noticed that Ivan came in early and stayed late several times this week. He appeared to be hard at work at his desk and on the phone several days.	
	3/1	Vacation scheduled March 1–5. However, Ivan was well aware that the Request for Proposal was due on the first and therefore prior to his vacation. This delay caused a ripple effect across the department.	This is a concern. Talk to Ivan about this.
	3/8	Ivan received kudos from customer Mary Victors. She is pleased with the software suite sold to her.	
	3/15	I overheard Ivan using foul language with a customer. We spoke shortly thereafter.	

APPENDIX II

Sample Performance Log (B)
(Calendar)

					Recorded by Susan Henderson, Supervisor	

MARCH 2006

Performance Calendar

Ivan M. Goode

Sun	Monday	Tuesday	Wednesday	Thursday	Friday	Sat
			1 Executive Search Co. purchased more Acme products. Ivan was the lead on this sale.	**2**	**3** Kudos from customer Mary Victors to Ivan. She is pleased with the software suite sold to her.	**4**
5	**6**	**7**	**8** IVAN ON VACATION THIS WEEK	**9**	**10**	**11**
12	**13**	**14** Ivan's sales revenues are impressive again as noted on the quarterly report.	**15** I overheard Ivan using foul language with a customer.	**16** The outline for the Request for Proposal is overdue.	**17**	**18**
19	**20** Ivan offered very good comments to the software developers on the roll out of the beta version. Good salespeople know their products. Ivan knew his products and what was needed to support them.	**21**	**22**	**23**	**24** Ivan was kind to assist Roger with the proper method of using our new sales tracking software.	**25**
26	**27**	**28** Progress Review held.	**29**	**30** **Mom's Birthday**	**31** Ivan came early and stayed late several times this week. Appeared to be working hard on the phone.	

www.performanceconversations.com

Appendix III

Sample Performance Log (C)
(E-Mail and 7 x 7 Method)
From Employee

| GET MAIL | SEND MAIL | REPLY | REPLY ALL | DELETE | FORWARD | PRINT |

Subject: Weekly 7x7 Report—Week of May 8th
From: I. M. Goode <igoode@acmeproduce.com>
To: Susan Henderson <shenderson@acmeproduce.com>
Date: 5/12/2006 4:32 p.m.

Susan:

Here is the report of my week's activities:

- Successfully closed on sale of new version of ERP software to two existing clients.
- Made appointments for all sales calls for the month of June.
- Updated my contact list of 2005 leads.
- Completed my review of the specifications for beta-tested 2007 models.
- Attended an online seminar on the "The Art of the Close" selling technique.
- Got a thank you note from Mary Victors. She really likes using the new products we sold her in February. She says that her revenues are up.
- I did not complete the Request for Proposal outline as scheduled. I did not have enough information at my fingertips, so I will work on it next week.

Next week, I will spend the majority of the time completing my quarterly budget. I will take PTO time on Thursday afternoon since I have a doctor's appointment. Nonetheless, here are my planned activities:

- Complete quarterly budget before the June 1st deadline.
- Meet with Tyler Smith about new deadlines for software implementation.
- Complete the executive search RFP.
- Make initial calls to all remaining 2005 leads.

If you have any questions about my progress on the assignments we discussed last month, please let me know. I look forward to speaking with you next week at our regular meeting.

Sincerely,

Ivan M. Goode

Appendix IV

Sample Performance Log (D)
(Journal)

Supervisor Log

Friday, May 12, 2006

Ivan Goode—Ivan continues to do well on all sales related activities. He is ahead of last year's totals and ahead of the projections for the next quarter. Selling is his "strong suit." However, he does not like following through with all of the sales documentation as he should.

Roger Smith—Fernando Ortez called to place orders for 2007 and noted how much he enjoys working with Roger Smith. He seemed to indicate that a lot of his patronage has to do with a good relationship with all Acme customer service associates. It appears that Roger has done a good job of working with Mr. Ortez over the past two years.

Becky Gunderson—I tried to reach Becky Gunderson on the phone three times today and she did not answer her office or her cell phone. I left several messages for her to call me.

Monday, May 15, 2006

Becky Gunderson—she was a little abrupt on the phone with me today as I reminded her that I needed all budgets for the third quarter by June 1 as scheduled. This appears to be a pattern. Becky seems to react negatively to any reminders of when her requirements are due. This would not be an issue except that she routinely misses deadlines by a day or so. The deadlines are never long, but they are routinely missed. She has asked for another day or for the "weekend" to complete assignments on several occasions.

Thursday, May 18, 2006

Ivan M. Goode—Quarterly budget submitted in advance. Good job.

Quarterly sales revenues have exceeded all projections. Everyone on my team deserves credit for the great results.

Virginia Billingsley—Last week's weekly report was received today.

Appendix V

Sample Performance Portfolio Contents

(Evidence of efforts, behaviors, and results)

Optional Contents in a Typical Performance Portfolio

◊ Supervisor's Performance Logs, calendars, journals, e-mails, etc.

◊ Employee's Performance Logs, calendars, journals, e-mails, etc.

◊ Reports (any departmental or organizational reports of outcomes, i.e. quarterly sales report)

◊ E-mail from satisfied customer

◊ Outline of completed *action plan* for next quarter

◊ Supervisor notes from third-party conversations (complaints, thank-you notes, discussions, etc.)

◊ Notes supervisor kept from discussion with peers about employee's collegiality and teamwork

◊ Completed To Do lists

◊ Photocopy of training certificate

◊ Photocopy of awards or other recognition

◊ Letter of reprimand, discipline, etc.

◊ Thank you notes from peer, customer, supervisor, other.

◊ Photocopy of completed reports (or cover page of reports)

◊ Statistics that indicate work accomplished

◊ Picture of completed project, item, report, or device etc.

◊ Company reports on collective activities of division, department, or section in which employee belongs. Departmental successes are individual successes and vice versa.

◊ Evidence of positive publicity for employee's effort

◊ Photocopy of the cover page of a project

◊ Statistics

◊   Articles, publications, brochures

◊   Work samples

◊   Anything that documents efforts, behaviors or results

◊   Any document that describes work accomplished, attempted, or not achieved

Tip: The Performance Portfolio can be held by either the employee or the supervisor. In either case, the employee should have unrestricted access to the Performance Portfolio at all times. It is an ideal scenario for the employee to have all of the evidence that characterizes their efforts available to them at all times. This way the employee always knows where he or she "stands" with regard to performance. The Performance Portfolio is a form of instant feedback.

Appendix VI

Progress Review Checklist
(And Guidelines)

PERFORMANCE CONVERSATIONS® ARE OPERATIONAL. They involve discussions about what is needed to get the job done or ensure it gets done correctly and on time.

◊ The progress review should be scheduled

◊ Supervisor's Performance Log, calendar, or journal, etc. should be updated prior to meeting.

◊ Employee has completed their Performance Log, calendar, journal, etc.—and has otherwise prepared.

◊ Establish rapport and an atmosphere of partnership.

Tip: Use "we" instead of "you" or "I" as much as possible.

◊ Discussion centers upon the content of Performance Logs and the Performance Portfolio.

◊ Discuss the status of short-term performance goals made at latest Progress Review.

◊ Discuss progress made on long-term, or annual goals, projects, etc., as appropriate.

◊ Obstacles to success identified and addressed.

◊ Acknowledge, recognize, congratulate, or give employee *pat on the back* for good efforts, behaviors, and outcomes.

◊ Address, discuss, problem-solve performance aberrations, shortfalls, errors, omissions, or failures. Talk about the "bad" stuff. Don't avoid it. Deal with it while it is small.

◊ Agree upon steps necessary for improvement.

◊ Negotiate options to deal with performance challenges. Gain buy-in for action plans/solutions.

◊ Ask questions—wait and listen for answers. Supervisor attempts to listen more than they talk.

◊   Evaluate performance information, data, or evidence.

Tip: Ask the employee to assist you in interpreting all the available information and evidence. Ask him or her, "What does it mean?" or "How does this information compare with our goals, standards, or the plans that were previously agreed upon?"

◊   Employee is asked if there is anything else that should be discussed before wrapping-up the conversation.

◊   Thank the employee for his or her participation and remind him or her of your shared goals and responsibilities for outcomes.

◊   Determine who will draft notes or document this Progress Review.

The general discussion should include at least these three elements:

1) *Celebrate* those things that appear on both logs—this is an indication that there is a mutual understanding of appropriate performance requirements and performance indicators.

2) *Recognize* those things that the employee tracked that the supervisor did not know or forgot. The supervisor benefits from this information by (a) learning of the employee's efforts, (b) recognizing or rewarding the efforts uncovered, (c) having the opportunity of redirecting efforts from those items mentioned to things that are a higher priority at this time, if necessary.

3) *Emphasize* those things that the supervisor saw as important and draw the employee's attention to things on the supervisor's log, which might be a higher priority.

Sample Progress Review Summaries

Sample one—Bullet Format

Progress Review

March 11, 2006

Susan and I met during our regularly scheduled check-in and all appears well. There were several major topic areas discussed during our meeting:

- She noted that my major area of strength was actually selling.
- My recent sales reports are evidence of my success.
- We talked about the need for me to do better on completing my paperwork.
- I gave a progress update on my yearly goals, I am ahead on most projects.
- There are several professional development opportunities that I should consider pursuing.
- My Performance Portfolio included several kudos. One from a coworker and two from customers.

I did not have any major problems or challenges at this time.
Ivan M. Goode

Sample two – Narrative Format

Progress Review

March 11, 2006

At the most recent progress review, Ivan and I met to discuss a variety of trends that have developed over the recent two-month period. During this time it has become increasingly apparent that his greatest asset is his ability to close the sale. He has performed well on selling existing products, new products, and has done well selling follow-on products such as upgrades. He has received compliments from upper management via the quarterly sales results, and from coworkers and customers. Ivan continues to do well in all areas except his follow-up paperwork. We discussed the need for him to concentrate more in this area. He is interested in more professional development opportunities and will attend some training in the coming months.

Overall, Ivan is doing a good job and is an asset to the Sales department. We will review his progress on yearly goals more closely at the next progress review.

GOOD JOB Ivan. Keep up the good work.

Susan Henderson

Tip: (1) The summary of the progress review should be as simple as possible and always less than one page of content. (2) The supervisor and subordinate should alternate taking notes of these meetings. (3) When the progress review is filled with a number of negative items, it is a good idea to require the employee to write the notes from the meeting to ensure that he or she understands the items upon which they should focus their attention.

Appendix VIII

Annual Performance Analysis and Summary Checklist
(And Guidelines)

THE PURPOSE OF THE annual performance analysis and summary checklist is three-fold: (1) to analyze important information, (2) to identify positive and negative trends, (3) to start anew the process of planning for future successes.

◊ Ensure Performance Portfolio is updated with all supervisor's and subordinate's Performance Logs, calendars, journals, lists, etc.

◊ Review all the summaries from the progress reviews.

◊ Take time to think about, synthesize, analyze, and appreciate the overall content of the Performance Portfolio prior to meeting with the employee.

• Make notes as appropriate.

• Identify positive trends and outcomes.

• Identify negative trends, actions, or outcomes.

◊ Give the employee the Performance Portfolio and ask them to review the content and make notes in preparation for the annual performance discussion.

◊ Discuss major ideas, projects, events, accomplishments, successes, or errors.

◊ Take the opportunity to recognize the employee's successes, as appropriate.

◊ Reprimand the employee as appropriate.

◊ Gain commitment and agreement to improve as appropriate.

◊ Start the process of planning for next year.

◊ Identify goals, challenges, and obstacles.

◊ Rededicate oneself to the mission of the organization.

◊ Rededicate oneself to the partnership of supervisor and subordinate working together.

◊   Acknowledge the past, but create plans to work together to create a mutually beneficial future.

◊   Determine if the employee has any professional development goals. Plan a separate meeting to discuss professional development.

◊   Create action plans to achieve work goals and professional development goals.

Tip: Simple plans are best. They should contain a limited number of goals and the goals must be: (1) specific and easily defined, (2) specific as to assignment— who must take action to accomplish the goals, and (3) by what date the action will be taken.

◊   Thank the employee for being a part of the team.

◊   Forecast the next meeting and the schedule of upcoming progress reviews.

Appendix IX

Sample Performance Questions
(For Supervisors and Subordinates)

Here are some sample questions that can be used to stimulate dialogue during Progress Reviews:

1. Have you had time to prepare for this performance conversation? *(If not, stop and reschedule the meeting. Ensure that he or she understands that when the meeting resumes, the conversation will consist of two-way communication and participation.)*

2. Do you know what is expected of you?

3. Do you know how your work integrates with others?

4. Do you know why what you do every day matters?

5. Do you know how your work is connected to the company's mission?

6. Are you getting enough support at work from coworkers, manager, etc.?

7. Are there things that I (the supervisor) am not aware of that limit your ability to do your best work?

8. Have you had any workplace related problems since our last discussion?

9. How are things going?

10. Are we making progress on the goals that we previously discussed?

11. What can I (the supervisor) do to help you do your job better?

12. What are two things that I (or you) should stop doing?

13. What are two things I (or you) should start doing?

14. What are two things I (or you) should keep doing?

15. Are there things that I say that are not the same as the things that I do?

16. Do you have talents that you could utilize on the job that I (the supervisor) do not know about?

17. What are you most proud of accomplishing over the past few weeks (month or year)?

18. Are you enjoying your work?

19. What information or evidence do you have that illustrates that you are doing a good job?

20. Are we tracking the right information about what you do everyday?

21. How do you know at the end of the day that you have done a good job?

22. What responsibilities that you and I jointly share that we are not getting done?

23. What performance related information could help us understand how well you are doing at work that we do not have at this time?

24. Am I missing anything that we should talk about?

25. Are there important work-related issues that you are reluctant to talk about for some reason, to talk about at this time, or to talk about with me?

26. Do you have any questions for me?

Tip: It is a good practice to give the employee these questions prior to a performance conversation. The list will serve as a tickler for them to think about the type of operational issues that they would like to discuss when they meet with you.

Appendix X

Performance Discussion Ideas
(For Employees)

Here are some ideas for employees to think about in advance of a progress review or annual performance analysis and summary session. This checklist helps the employee to prepare for these meetings.

◊ What evidence do I have that shows that I have been performing in the manner that was agreed upon?

◊ What are the things that have I have been doing that my supervisor does not know about?

◊ Are there problems with my tools, workstation, equipment, supplies, or resources?

◊ Are there any issues with coworkers, customers, vendors, or others that have affected my ability to do all of my work?

◊ Do I have personal challenges that have affected or might affect my work?

◊ Is my job description up-to-date?

◊ Are my job requirements clear? Do I know what is expected of me?

◊ What progress have I made on short-term and long term goals?

◊ What can the supervisor do to help me do my job better?

◊ What are the things that I am most proud of in recent weeks (months, year)?

◊ Have I received any thank-you notes or kudos from others lately?

◊ What training have I participated in, or what new skills have I learned?

◊ What are the major challenges or obstacles that prevent me from doing an even better job than I am doing?

◊ Do I have any skills that are not being fully utilized in my work?

◊ What are my self-improvement goals for the coming year?

◊   What are the ideas that I have about improving our department's operations?

◊   Which of my coworkers have supported me well lately?

Reference List

Allender, H. D. (1995). Reengineering employee performance appraisals the TQM way. Total quality management. Institute of Industrial Engineers, Inc. From E-library.com.

Amabile, T. M. (September–October 1998). How to kill creativity, *Harvard Business Review*. 77–87.

Bain, V. (2001). Individual performance isn't a solo activity. *The Journal for Quality and Participation*. www.aqp.org.

Baldwin, T. T., Ford, J. K. (1988). Transfer of training: a review and directions for future research. *Personnel Psychology*. 41: 63–105.

Benham, P. (May 17, 2004). Letter to the author.

—— (2001). Performance appraisal: A radical view. *The 2001 Annual Review:* (Vol. 2, Consulting). Jossey-Bass/Pfeiffer.

Bennis, W., (September–October 1972). Chairman Mac in perspective. *Harvard Business Review.*

Blanchard, K. and R. Lorber. (1984). *Putting the one-minute manager to work.* New York: William Morrow and Company, Inc.

Blancard, K., Zigarmi, P., Zigarmi, D. (1989). *Leadership and the one minute manager: increasing effectiveness through situational leadership.* New York: William Morrow and Company, Inc.

Belak, T. (2003). *Performance appraisals: are you "punishing" with paper or charting a course for the stars.* Louisville, Kentucky: Transformata Publishing.

Bowen, R. B. (2000). *Recognizing and rewarding employees.* McGraw-Hill Trade.

Bowman, J. S. (1999). *Performance appraisal: verisimilitude trumps veracity.* Alexandria, Virginia: Public Personnel Management, International Personnel Management Association.

Buckingham, M., and Coffman, C. (1999). *First, break all the rules: what the world's greatest managers do differently.* Simon and Schuster.

Burke, M. E., and Esen, E. (January 2005). *Workplace productivity*. Alexandria, Virginia: Society for Human Resource Management Research Division.

Carson, K., Cardy, R., Dobbins, G. (June 1991). Performance appraisal as effective management or deadly management disease. *Group and Organizational Studies*. 143–158.

Clifford, P. (1999). *The collective wisdom of the workforce: conversations with public personnel management*. Alexandria, Virginia: International Personnel Management Association.

Coens, T. (March 2000). Say goodbye to performance appraisals (really!) and hello to a happier, more productive workplace. *American Society for Quality, Annual Spring Conference Proceedings*. vol. 22, O: 1–10. Orlando, FL.

Coens, T. and Jenkins, M. (2002). *Abolishing performance appraisals: why they backfire and what to do instead*. San Francisco: Berrett-Koehler Publishers, Inc.

Cook, J. (1999). *Effective coaching*. McGraw-Hill, Inc.

Costello, S. J. (1994). *Effective performance management*. McGraw-Hill Companies, Inc.

Day, C. M. (1991). A hard look at performance reviews: techniques in handling medical personnel. *Medical Laboratory Observer*. Nelson Publishing, Inc., Nokomis, FL.

Deming, W. E. (1986). *Out of crisis*. Cambridge: MIT Press.

Deblieux, M. (2003). *Performance appraisal source book: a collection of practical samples*. Alexandria, Virginia: Society for Human Resource Management.

Drake, J. D. (1998). *Performance appraisals: one more time*. Menlo Park, CA: Crisp Publications.

Drumm, G. (April 1998). The why, what, and how of performance management. *American Society for Quality, Annual Spring Conference Proceedings*. (Vol. 20). 0: 457–469.

Farson, R. and R. Keyes. (2002). *The innovation paradox: the success of failure, the failure of success*. New York: Free Press.

Fournies, F. F. (1999). *Coaching for improved work performance*, rev. ed. McGraw-Hill Trade.

——(1999). *Why employees don't do what they are supposed to do.* McGraw-Hill Books.

Friedman-Fixler, J. (March 2003). *Volunteer valuation, not evaluation.* Volunteer Management Review. Retrieved November 2, 2005. www.charitychannel.com/publish/templates/?a=1189andz=24.

Glover, R. B. (November 1996). Why are we ignoring performance appraisal research? *Parks and Recreation*; National Recreation and Parks Association. (Vol. 31, Issue 11). 24 -28.

Green, P. (1999). *Building robust competencies: linking human resources systems to organizational strategies.* Jossey-Bass, Inc., San Francisco.

Grote, R. C. (1995). *Discipline without punishment: the proven strategy that turns problem employees into superior performers.* New York: AMACOM.

Hackman, J., and Oldman, G. (1975). Motivation through the design of work. *Organisational Behaviour and Human Performance.* 16: 250-279.

Harvard Business Review on Motivating People. (2003). Cambridge: Harvard Business School Press.

Henderson, R. I. (1997). *Compensation management in a knowledge-based world.* 7th ed., Upper Saddle River, N.J.

Hendricks, W. (1994). *The manager's role as a coach.* Shawnee Mission, Kansas: National Press Publications.

Hershey. P. (1985). *The situational leader.* Warner Books.

Herzberg, F. (2003). How do you motivate employees. *Harvard Business Review on Motivating People.* Cambridge: Harvard Business School Press.

Johnson, M. A. and Kaupins, G. E. (January-February 1992). Keeping lies out of the performance appraisal. *Industrial Management.* (Vol. 34, No. 1). 6–8.

Katzenbach, J. R. (2003). *Why pride matters more than money: the power of the worlds' greatest motivational force.* New York: Crown Business.

Kirkpatrich, D. (1982). *How to improve performance through appraisal and coaching.* New York: AMACOM.

Kohn, A. (1993). *Punished by rewards: the trouble with gold stars, incentive plans, A's, praise and other bribes.* Boston: Houghton Mifflin Co.

Knight, M. E., Gallaro, D. (1994). *Portfolio assessment: applications for portfolio analysis.* Lanham, Maryland: University Press of America.

Langdon, D. (2002). *Aligning performance: improving people, systems, and organizations.* San Francisco: Josey-Bass/Pfeiffer.

Laurel, D. S. (2003). User friendly performance management. *Performance Appraisal: Perspectives on a Quality Management Approach.* Laurel and Associates, Ltd. University of Minnesota Training and Development Research Center and The American Society for Training And Development Research Committee, 1990.

Lecky-Thompson, R. (1999). *Constructive appraisals.* Washington, D.C.: American Management Association.

Levinson, H. (2003). Management by whose objectives. *Harvard Business Review on Motivating People.* Cambridge: Harvard Business School Press.

Maddux, R. B. (1987). *Effective performance appraisals.* rev. ed. Los Altos, California: Crisp Publications Inc.

Markle, G. L. (2000). *Catalytic coaching—the end of the performance review.* Westport, Connecticut: Quorum Books.

Mariotti, J. (1997). Tough bosses, easy bosses. (employee performance evaluation). *Industry Week.*

Mathis, R. L., Jackson, J. H. (2003). *Human resource management.* 10th ed. Mason, Ohio: Thomson-Southwestern.

Maurer, R. (1994). *The feedback toolkit: 16 tools for better communication in the workplace.* Portland, Oregon: Productivity Press.

McGregor, D. (September–October 1972). An uneasy look at performance appraisal. *Harvard Business Review.* Cambridge: Harvard Business School Press.

McKirchy, K. (1994). *How to conduct win-win performance appraisals.* Shawnee Mission, Kansas: National Press Publications.

Minor, M. (1989). *Coaching and counseling.* Los Altos: Crisp Publications Inc.

Neal, Jr., J. E. (2001). *The #1 guide to performance appraisals: doing it right.* Perrysburg, Ohio: Neal Publications Inc.

Nelson, B. (1994). *1001 ways to reward employees.* New York: Workman Publishing Company.

Nicholson, N. (2003). How to motivate your problem people. *Harvard business review on motivating people.* Cambridge: Harvard Business School Press

Noe, R. A., Hollenbeck, J. R., Gerhart, B., Wright, P. M. (2006). *Human resources management: gaining a competitive advantage,*·5th ed. Boston: Irwin, McGraw-Hill.

Pfeffer-Stanford, J. (May–June 1998) Six dangerous myths about pay. *Harvard Business Review*; Cambridge, MA. 109-119.

Ripley, D. (May 1999). Improving employee performance: moving beyond traditional HRM responses. Retrieved December 15, 2004 from www.ispi.org/services/suggestedreading.htm.

Roberts, G.E. (2002). Employee performance appraisal system participation: a technique that works, *Public Personnel Management*. (Vol. 31 No.3). 333–42.

Robinson, J. C., Robinson, D. G. (2001). *Shifting from training to performance: what smart trainers know*. San Francisco: Jossey-Bass/Pfeiffer.

Robinson, J. (1995). *How to conduct employees performance appraisals*. Walnut Creek, California: Council On Education in Management, Institute for International Research.

Sartain, L., Finney, M. I. (2003). *HR from the heart: inspiring stories and strategies for building the people side of great business*. American Management Association.

Schein, E. (1993). *Organizational culture and leadership in classics of organization theory*. Edited by Jay Shafritz and J. Steven Ott. Fort Worth: Harcourt College Publishers.

Strodel, N. (2004). Letter to the author.

Tetreault, R. (2004). Letter to the author.

Thottam, J. (January 17, 2007). Thank God it's Monday. *Time*. A58–A61.

Wycoff, J. (June 2003). The "big 10" innovations killers: how to keep your innovation system alive and well. *Journal for Quality and Participation*. (Vol. 26). 2:17-22.

Index

About the Author

Christopher D. Lee, PhD, SPHR

CHRIS LEE IS A human resources practitioner, lecturer, researcher, and author. He has served as the chief human resources officer for three different colleges or universities, and a state college system. Formerly a question writer for the *PHR* and *SPHR* examinations administered by the Human Resources Certification Institute (HRCI), he is currently a member of its Exam Review Panel.

His areas of expertise are employment, training, and performance management—or, in his words, "finding, developing, and managing talent in organizations." He is the author of a book called *Search Committees*, which is a guide to the hiring process for colleges and universities. He has written other works entitled *Rethinking the Goals of Your Performance Management Process* and *Conversations, Not Evaluations: An Alternate Model of Performance Management*.

He is a frequent presenter at national, regional, and local conferences for the Society for Human Resource Management (SHRM) and the College of University Professional Association for Human Resources (CUPA-HR). Additionally, he is an active professional and holds or has held leadership positions in local, state, and national human resources organizations. Chris earned a master's degree in human resource management, a doctor of philosophy degree in human resource development, and he is also certified as a Senior Professional in Human Resources.

For more information on the Performance Conversations® Model or to host a training seminar for managers in your organization, please go to www.performanceconversations.com.

Printed in the United States
219812BV00001B/38/A

9 781587 366055